WHITE
WORKING
CLASS

WHITE WORKING CLASS

*Overcoming
Class Cluelessness
in America*

Joan C. Williams

HARVARD BUSINESS REVIEW PRESS

BOSTON, MASSACHUSETTS

Copyright 2020 Joan C. Williams
All rights reserved
Printed in the United States of America

10 9 8 7 6 5 4 3 2 1

No part of this publication may be reproduced, stored in or introduced into a retrieval system, or transmitted, in any form, or by any means (electronic, mechanical, photocopying, recording, or otherwise), without the prior permission of the publisher. Requests for permission should be directed to permissions@harvardbusiness.org, or mailed to Permissions, Harvard Business School Publishing, 60 Harvard Way, Boston, Massachusetts 02163.

The web addresses referenced in this book were live and correct at the time of the book's publication but may be subject to change.

Library of Congress Cataloguing-in-Publication data is forthcoming.

ISBN: 978-1-63369-821-5

eISBN: 978-1-63369-822-2

The paper used in this publication meets the requirements of the American National Standard for Permanence of Paper for Publications and Documents in Libraries and Archives Z39.48-1992.

To my children,
with hopes for their future

Equality means dignity. And dignity demands a job and a paycheck that lasts through the week.

—Dr. Martin Luther King, Jr.

I have been repeatedly mocked for trying to explain how my neighbors feel and why they feel the way they do. Racism, sexism, and a fear of both Islam and Latin[os] are present. So is a fear of not being able to feed children, not being able to take care of elderly loved ones, not being able to maintain dignity in the face of layoff after layoff. Yes, I'm sick and tired of humoring the white male working class. That doesn't mean their economic and political concerns should be ignored. It doesn't mean it's OK to laugh at us for trying to maintain our rural lifestyle. Some of us live on land that our great-great-grandparents cultivated. Final point: my family is multiracial, and I am full of rage, fear, and heartbreak over the dangers that many of us are now in because of this election. My fellow "liberals" should have listened to those of us they call hillbillies, rednecks, hicks, and toothless idiots. They should have understood we don't live in a "fly-over" state; we live in our home.

—Erin Brown

Contents

Foreword

Too many Americans feel that Washington has turned its back on them. They know they work hard, and they believe that anyone who works hard in America deserves to earn a stable middle-class life—at least. Whether you're a Democrat, independent, or Republican, you need to understand the depth of the anger that is driving American politics today. And you need to understand the reason for that anger.

I grew up in Pittsburgh, in a traditional blue-collar family. My dad did car upholstery—he didn't love it, but it supported the family. My parents scrimped to save money, but we always had the basics: a house, a car that worked. My parents worked hard, and their hard work paid off. They took pride in their work ethic and their ability to persevere.

Joan Williams's book is truly enlightening. It describes the values I was raised with: self-reliance, hard work, stability, and straight talk. It also answers the questions many people have been asking about the so-called white working class since Trump was elected in 2016. (They're the middle class, by the way.) Why are they so angry? Why is so much of their anger focused on government? Why don't they just move to where the jobs are? Why don't they get their act together and go to college? Joan Williams answers these questions and more.

Most important, she shows that Americans want a country where hard work pays off. They will collect government benefits or go on disability—if that's what they need to do to support their families. But that's not what they *want*. They want what my parents had: the ability to work hard and create a stable family life.

When I was in high school and still trying to figure out if and how I could afford to go to college, my mom recommended that I learn how to lay carpet, because she was concerned about my future. Her goal was not that I find fulfillment but that I find stability—the kind of stability that has become so elusive in the era of closed-down factories, abandoned Main Streets, and the opioid epidemic. It turned out I wasn't very good with carpet but did have a knack for starting technology businesses. But here's the fact: not everyone is an entrepreneur, and not everyone has a direct path to a job that can pay their bills.

As much as I believe that the American dream is alive and well, my experience in business has taught me that not everyone lives in a situation conducive to chasing that dream that so many of us have taken for granted.

I've been in situations where I've come home to find my utilities turned off. Where I didn't have money to pay for health care and, even worse, had to go to a dental clinic where student dentists botched my root canal—and then their efforts to fix their mistakes made it even worse. I have written checks and then scrambled to figure out how to cover them before they bounced. But I was fortunate: I only had to take care of myself. I didn't have to worry about a spouse or children or providing for others in my family. I was able to move to Dallas, living with five roommates in a three-bedroom apartment, and get a bartending job at night and a sales job during the day, which allowed me to get my head above water.

Today, most people don't have the luxury of mobility. They are reluctant to move for a better job because that's very risky in their world. They stick close to home because a small network of family and friends they've known forever sustains them both economically and emotionally. That network provides child care, elder care, help fixing the car— necessities of life they can't take for granted. Equally important, that network offers blue-collar families something not on offer from their less-than-prestigious jobs: respect.

I've been at the top, among the 1 percent that are truly financially blessed. And I've been at the bottom. Broke. Scrambling to make ends meet.

Anyone who's willing to get up every day, and show up and work hard—that person has my respect. Disrespect breeds anger, and anger distorts politics. Treating working-class people with the respect they deserve is not a partisan issue. Making sure that hard work pays off in America is not a partisan issue.

Our politics are being driven by middle-class people's fear of falling into poverty. We need to stop scolding people for being afraid, or for expressing their fears the wrong way. We need to listen to them. In this book, Joan Williams does just that. She gives a voice to those who get up every day and do their best, and she lets them explain how American politics got to where it is today.

Their voices will open your eyes—and hopefully your heart and mind as well.

Mark Cuban

Preface

It's been quite a ride. In the 18 months after the publication of *White Working Class*, I spent more time in the halls of Congress than I did in the 25 years I lived in DC. The full range of Democrats and progressives, from Joe Biden to Nancy Pelosi to Bernie Sanders to Kamala Harris, listened to me with apparent attentiveness. I addressed both the House and the Senate committees in charge of Democrats' messaging. I knew I was making progress when one congressman asked me fervently, "Do you know that *two-thirds* of Americans don't have college degrees?" When I first started spouting that statistic, no one in my circle would believe it. *Everyone* they knew had college degrees.

To my surprise, the book also has been influential outside the United States, wherever people are trying to make sense of economic populism. There's a Japanese edition, and I have addressed legislators from the House of Lords in the United Kingdom, as well as the Danish and Dutch parliaments and policymakers and journalists from the European Union, Canada, Denmark, Sweden, Australia, New

Zealand, the Netherlands, and France. With the train wreck that is Brexit, pundits in the United Kingdom are especially obsessed with trying to understand working-class anger, ranging from the *Guardian* to the *Financial Times*.

Not surprisingly, the growing acknowledgment of the role of class resentment in contemporary politics has been accompanied by resistance. Acknowledging social privilege is never fun, and acknowledging the influence of social class is particularly unsettling to a global elite convinced that its success reflects merit, not privilege. People tend to resist whenever their core identities are threatened.

Conversations with Europeans reflect a long tradition, only recently withered, of class analysis, from Marx to Gramsci. The United States lacks this tradition, and it shows. Resistance to my message in the United States has been fed, too, by a narrative that posits a zero-sum game between race and class. Interestingly, there's no sense that one can't support both trans rights and racial justice, or both immigrant rights and gender justice. So it's unclear why racial equity and class equity are seen as mutually exclusive.

They aren't. My own research on engineers found that while only one-third of white men report discriminatory standards, two-thirds of people of color do.[1] Race is important in professional jobs, but so is class. As one reader wrote to me, "Being a 'class migrant' is a struggle that never seems to end." The research backs her up. One study found that men from elite backgrounds received invitations to interview at top-ranked law firms at more than 12 times the rate of their equally qualified, working-class peers.[2] Measures that would help level the playing field for women and people of color in professional jobs—check them out at BiasInterrupters.org—also would help class migrants of all races.

Resistance also reflects the calls to abandon identity politics, forwarded by well-meaning authors such as Mark Lilla.[3] Although I find much of Lilla's analysis compelling, I and many others find his call to abandon identity politics irritating. After forty years of largely ineffectual diversity efforts, white men from elite backgrounds still dominate high-stakes, high-status jobs at the top of every industry. So now we're supposed to move on?

Class is an identity; let's make it count. The harsh disdain of elites feeds working-class anger. I am sometimes shocked by the response to my writings: "I wish all these [white working-class] people would die, frankly . . . They are mostly obese and some of them use opiates. They also have guns that they can kill themselves with. It can't happen soon enough for me," one reader wrote me.

We've tried to work on other vectors of social equality while ignoring class. It hasn't worked. Predictably, the public discourse that depicts white men as privileged is infuriating to blue-collar families in an era when noncollege men's wages fell precipitously. A lot more research has emerged documenting this since the initial publication of *White Working Class*. The Economic Policy Institute has shown that, though wages rose when productivity did in the decades after World War II, that ascent ended in the 1970s; if it had continued, wages would be *twice* what they are today.[4]

Raj Chetty and his coauthors have documented that, while virtually every American born in the 1940s did better than their parents, only about half of Americans born in the 1980s do.[5] It's no response to say that working-class whites only achieved the American dream after World War II due to white privilege. That's true, but irrelevant—surely the point is not that whites deserved to lose access to the American dream but that both people of color *and* whites deserve to gain access to it.

American workers know they've been screwed: they see it in rusted factories, despair deaths, sped-up lives patching together part-time, dead-end jobs. The far right, with considerable success, has encouraged whites to interpret their sharp loss of status through the lens of whiteness, with a consequent rise in open racism.[6] The challenge is to explain to the white working class that they have gotten screwed not because they are *white* but because they are *working class*. The sooner we start, the better.

This lesson is not limited to the left: misdirected economic populism is not working for conservatives either. The clearest example is Brexit. Cooler heads from both the right and the left need to create a return to economic opportunity as well as new feeling rules that stigmatize derision of all disadvantaged groups. This is not just a possibility—I actually accomplished it. In the course of a single week on tour, I did both an hour-long podcast for left-leaning *Slate* and an appearance on *Fox News*, with positive feedback from both. All I did was point out the need for family-sustaining jobs and respect for the dignity of blue-collar men. And I thought: really, how hard is this?

I happen to be writing this from China, where I'm the tagalong spouse accompanying my husband, an expert on privacy and cybersecurity. His descriptions of China made me determined to go, in part because it's a country with a long history of the kind of geographical maldistribution of opportunity that the United States developed only recently. Jack Ma's response was to create Alibaba, a tech company that's a combined eBay, Amazon, and PayPal. While the concentration of so much power is sobering, there are bright spots: a subsidiary trains rural Chinese to use their e-platform to sell agricultural goods and handicrafts to the world, bringing opportunity and talent back into rural areas.

Similar transformation is possible here. What if an electrician in Indiana could use a smart helmet to fix a machine in Thailand? Or if a company in Mississippi could use 3-D printing to sell customized prosthetics worldwide? J. D. Vance (of *Hillbilly Elegy* fame) is financing new companies in the heartland, and money is pouring in to train tech talent in areas where young people can still afford to buy a house.[7] That's important, but tech talent is just a start.

An often-overlooked key to turning the tide of economic populism is to stop pretending that jobs fall fully formed from heaven. They don't. They're designed by people, who create either good, family-sustaining jobs or the kind of unstable jobs that have long demoralized the poor and are increasingly impoverishing the formerly middle class. Soon

60 percent of jobs will be at least partially automated.[8] We can design those as either good jobs or McJobs. If we go with McJobs, democracies—and businesses—will continue to pay in the coin of political instability.

The widespread assumption that there is a zero-sum game between addressing the concerns of the white working class and addressing the concerns of communities of color is demonstrably false. If we were to commit to providing good jobs for noncollege grads, that would help communities of color as well as working-class whites. For one thing, communities of color are more likely to be poor; for another, boys born to affluent black families are more likely to experience a fall in class status than their white peers.[9] College should be available and affordable to anyone with the drive and the inclination to go, but we also need community colleges to work with employers to help them identify the skills they need and to develop certificate programs employers trust and will therefore hire from. Such programs will also provide paths for formerly incarcerated people, points out Damon Phillips of Columbia Business School, who developed the ReEntry Acceleration Program (REAP) at the Tamer Center to enhance the job prospects of people who have served their sentences.[10]

A shift away from an exclusive focus on college is a transgressive suggestion in both the black and white communities. In the black community, Phillips points out, many African Americans have been taught since childhood that they need to be twice as good to get half as far, which has led blue-collar blacks to value education more than whites do.[11]

To question the indispensability of college is controversial, Phillips discovered in the course of his work at REAP. It's controversial in the white community, too: white elites' belief in the indispensability of college is integral to their belief that their success reflects a system that rewards the best and the brightest—them.

But providing a solid future without college is important, because when people lose touch with their hopes, they give way to their fears. No one is at their best when they're afraid. If you don't like the ugly face of fear, the only effective antidote is to provide hope by providing opportunity.

My own most fervent hope is to communicate one key message: if you care about climate change, or abortion rights, or immigrants, or mass incarceration, you'd better care, too, about good jobs and social dignity for Americans of all races without college degrees. Because if you don't, racialized economic populism is what you get.

Joan C. Williams
Hangzhou, China
March 2019

WHITE
WORKING
CLASS

1

Why Talk
About Class?

MY FATHER-IN-LAW GREW up eating blood soup. He hated it, whether because of the taste or the humiliation, I never knew. His alcoholic father regularly drank up the family wage, and the family was often short on food money. They were evicted from apartment after apartment.

He dropped out of school in eighth grade to help support the family. Eventually he got a good, steady job he truly hated, as an inspector in a factory that made those machines that measure humidity levels in museums. He tried to open several businesses on the side, but none worked, so he kept that job for 38 years. He rose from poverty to a middle-class life: the car, the house, two kids in Catholic school, the wife who worked only part time. He worked incessantly. He had two jobs in addition to his full-time position, one doing yard work for a local magnate and another hauling trash to the dump.

Throughout the 1950s and 1960s, he read *The Wall Street Journal* and voted Republican. He was a man before his time: a blue-collar white man who thought the union was a bunch of jokers who took your money and never gave you anything in return. Starting in the 1970s, many blue-collar whites followed his example.

Over the past 40-odd years, elites stopped connecting with the working class, whom prior generations had given a place of honor. Think of the idealized portrayals of noble blue-collar workers in post offices across the country, painted by artists of the Federal Art Project of the Works Progress Administration during the 1930s. (My favorite WPA mural is in Coit Tower in San Francisco.) Or of Tom Joad in John Steinbeck's *Grapes of Wrath* (1939), or Terry Malloy in the film *On the Waterfront* (1954). Elites worked hard to understand working-class men's striving and their pain.

Class consciousness has been replaced by class cluelessness—and in some cases, even class callousness. Emblematic of this reversal is "All in the Family," one of the most popular shows on television between 1971 and 1979. The central blue-collar character, Archie Bunker, represented a new and unflattering contrast to his long-haired, liberal, and enlightened college-going son-in-law. Archie was narrow-minded, coarse, ignorant, sexist, and racist. This image came from the core of the progressive elite: Norman Lear, the series producer, who later founded People for the American Way. The 1990s brought Al Bundy, the dimwitted women's shoe salesman on "Married … With Children," and Homer Simpson, who epitomized stereotypes of the working-class man as "crude, overweight, incompetent, clumsy, thoughtless and a border-line alcoholic" (to quote Wikipedia).[1] He works as an in-spector at a nuclear power plant, his laziness an ever-present danger to the environment.

With rare exceptions—Bruce Springsteen's lyrics come immediately to mind—this offensive portrait reigns today. It's unbecoming for a country that prides itself on a commit-ment to equality.

An entire book—a different one than mine—could seek to explain why this shift occurred. But the upshot is simply this: during an era when wealthy white Americans have learned to sympathetically imagine the lives of the poor, people of color, and LGBTQ people, the white working class has been insulted or ignored during precisely the period when their economic fortunes tanked. The typical white working-class household income doubled in the three decades after World War II but has not risen appreciably since.[2] The death rate for white working-class men—and women—aged 45-54 increased substantially between 1993 and 2013, a reversal from the de-cades before. In 1970, only a quarter of white children lived in neighborhoods with poverty rates of 10%; by 2000, 40% did.[3]

In an era when the economic fortunes of the white work-ing class plummeted, elites wrote off their anger as racism, sexism, nativism—beneath our dignity to take seriously. This has led us to politics polarized by working-class fury. "We're voting with our middle finger," said a Trump sup-porter in South Carolina.[4] If Trump fails to rejuvenate Flint, Michigan, and Youngstown, Ohio—and he probably will—things could turn even uglier. That's saying a lot.

This book focuses on the class comprehension gap that is allowing the United States (and Europe) to drift toward authoritarian nationalism. To be clear, I do not focus on hollow-eyed towns gutted by unemployment and the opioid epidemic, or despair deaths of white men with high school educations or less.[5] To focus on white working-class despair will lead well-meaning people to approach the white working class as they traditionally have approached the poor—as those "we have a moral and ethical obligation to help," to quote a well-meaning colleague. This attitude will infuriate them and only widen a societally unhealthy class divide.

Instead, I focus on a simple message: when you leave the two-thirds of Americans without college degrees out of your vision of the good life, they notice. And when elites commit to equality for many different groups but arrogantly dismiss "the dark rigidity of fundamentalist rural America,"[6] this is a recipe for extreme alienation among working-class whites. Deriding "political correctness" becomes a way for less-privileged whites to express their fury at the snobbery of more-privileged whites.

I don't like what this dynamic is doing to America. There are two reasons I think we have to try to replace it with a healthier one. The first is ethical: I am committed to social equality, not for some groups but for all groups. The second is strategic: the hidden injuries of class[7] now have become visible in politics so polarized that our democracy is threatened.

A few words about me. Nearly 40 years ago, I married a class migrant: someone who has moved from one class to another. My husband was born in a blue-collar family but then went to Harvard Law School. Myself, I'm a silver spoon girl, born and bred. My WASP father was from an affluent family that made its money in Chicago before returning home to Vermont. My mother was the German Jewish daughter of a well-known reform rabbi. I grew up in Princeton, went to Yale College, Harvard Law School, and MIT, and have been a law professor for nearly 40 years. I now live in San Francisco.

I still remember how, at 16, I fell madly in love with an Italian boy from Queens. I traveled to New York City from my hometown of Princeton, New Jersey, every weekend to go out with him, staying with my beloved grandmother on the Upper East Side. When he finally took me home to Bay Ridge for dinner, it didn't go well. His father seemed to hate me. His reaction: "She looked at us like a fucking anthropologist." I was cut to the quick, because it was so true.

The working class doesn't want to be examined like some tribe in a faraway land. They don't want the kind of pious solicitude the wealthy offer to the poor. (Perhaps the poor don't either; different topic.) They want respect for the lives they've built through unrelenting hard work. They want recognition for their contributions and their way of life. They keep our power lines repaired, our sewers functioning, our trains running. They give the mammograms that save our lives and pick us up off the street when we've been injured. They demand dignity—and they deserve it.

In the half-century since that painful dinner in Bay Ridge, I've come to understand that analyzing any group is best

handled with extreme caution. And even then, it can easily leave the analyzed feeling condescended to. Empathy—
something well-heeled and well-intentioned liberals often
call for as a way to cross the class divide—often reads as condescension. The hidden injuries of class are like a sunburn:
even a gentle touch can make you jump with outraged pain.

But we have to try. Or we will keep making the same mistakes that have helped foster the populist, anti-establishment
anger that welled up in the 2016 election. A good place to
start is with the common working-class phrase: "Born on
third base; thinks he hit a triple." Elites often pride ourselves
on merit, and point out we work very hard. But so do hotel
housekeepers. Let's not forget that.

Does renewed attention to the white working class mean
we should shift away from identity politics in favor of a
"post-identity liberalism"?[8] That's a silly idea: politics is always about identity, no less so for Donald Trump than Jesse
Jackson. One of the goals of this book is to help broaden the
conversation of identity to more deftly include class.

I've arranged the book around the kinds of questions
people tend to ask me, in blunt, private moments. Questions like, "Why doesn't the working class get with it and
go to college?" and "Why don't they just move to where
the jobs are?"

This book stems from a *Harvard Business Review* essay I
started on election night when I realized that Trump was
about to win the presidency. That essay, parts of which have
been woven into this book, has now been read millions of
times, and I've received hundreds of comments and emails

about it, many from people who had never written an author before. It was positively received by policymakers both on the left and on the right. Some of what they shared with me I've quoted in this book.[†] I have heard from people in Sweden, Australia, Germany, the Netherlands, the UK, Canada, Ireland, and Chile telling me that my comments about the U.S. white working class also describe something going on in their countries.

A friend wrote, "My working-class family expected Trump to win and for the most part, are quite hopeful about his presidency. My professional-class in-laws have written several emails about their immense grief over Clinton's loss. . . . I have found the difference in reactions astounding— and I think your article explains the reasons for it perfectly." I hope this book will help, too.

[†] Comments from the *HBR* website have a star (*). All comments are attributed using the handles used online. Quotations without citations are from personal emails or from conversations in which the person asked not to be identified. All quotations are used with permission.

CHAPTER 2

Who Is the
Working Class?

PRESUMABLY ON THE THEORY that no tree falls if no ear hears it, Americans curry a convenient deafness when it comes to class. A central way we make class disappear is to describe virtually everyone as "middle class." A recent *Bloomberg* story quoted an amusement park worker earning $22,000 a year and a lawyer with an annual income of $200,000, both calling themselves middle class.[9]

I still remember my shock when a close friend, a professor married to a partner in a major D.C. law firm, referred to herself as middle class. At the time, she undoubtedly belonged to the top 1%. And that lawyer who earns $200,000 a year? His income places him in the top 6% of American earners.[10] The working class is wise to such people: to working-class minds, lawyers (and doctors and bankers) aren't middle class. They are simply rich.

Objectively, the working class has a much better claim to middle-class standing. This becomes clearer when we seek out empirical data. In a study I coauthored with economist Heather Boushey of the Center for Equitable Growth, we defined Americans who are neither rich nor poor as those with household incomes above the bottom 30% but below the top 20%; then we added families with higher incomes but no college graduate.[11] This is the middle 53% of American families: the true middle class. As of 2015, these families had incomes ranging from $41,005 to $131,962. Their median income was $75,144. [12] At the high end are married families of, for example, a radiation therapist (median pay $70,010)[13] and a police officer (median pay $60,270).[14]

I had a lively discussion with my editor about what to call various groups in this book. I wanted to call the group in the middle the middle class, because, well, they *are*. My editor wisely pointed out that readers would be confused by that, if "middle class" is a term that we all use to describe ourselves regardless of whether it reflects reality. So I agreed to call those Americans in the middle—the ones who are neither rich nor poor—the "working class." But as part of the deal, I got to refer to the people at the top as an "elite." It's not a term many Americans are comfortable with, but if you are part of the professional-managerial class, well, you're an elite. Who composes this group? Americans with household incomes in the top 20% and at least one member who is a college graduate. The 2015 median income of such families was $173,175. Roughly 16.65% of American households fit this definition of the professional-managerial elite (PME).[15]

One reason the terms here are confusing is that when progressives use the phrase "the working class," they're often (though not always) using it as a euphemism for "poor." But the poor—in the bottom 30% of American families—are very different from Americans who are literally in the middle of the income distribution. With a median household income (in 2015) of $22,500,[16] low-income families typically have different family structures, different types of jobs, and different political beliefs from Americans in the middle. Only 12% of Trump voters have incomes below $30,000 a year—and Republicans are relatively rare among this group—something that bumps up the median income of Trump voters overall.[17]

Americans' failure to share a language to talk about class can leave us literally speechless on the topic. Or just plain wrong. Consider an influential article on the well-known website *FiveThirtyEight* in May 2016 titled, "The Mythology of Trump's Working Class Support." "It's been extremely common for news accounts to portray Donald Trump's candidacy as a 'working-class' rebellion against Republican elites," wrote Nate Silver. "His voters are better off economically compared with most Americans." While conceding "elements of truth" to the view that the working class was going for Trump, Silver attempted to disprove it by pointing out that the median income of Trump primary voters was $72,000, well above the national median of $56,000. But a household income of $72,000 is just a bit below the median working-class income, assuming you're using that term to refer to "working class" as neither rich nor poor.[18]

After the 2016 election, *FiveThirtyEight* gradually caught on. For statisticians, the best simple proxy for class is education. The strongest indicator of a Trump victory was a concentration of high-school-educated voters. Clinton's margin surged in the 50 most-educated counties and "collapsed" in the 50 least-educated, as compared with Obama's.[19]

Class cluelessness afflicts politicians as well as pundits. When progressive policymakers talk about guaranteeing things like paid sick leave or a higher minimum wage, they often frame them as issues that would help "working families." But neither offers what my father-in-law had: a steady job that yielded his vision of a middle-class life. That's what the working class still wants.

The reason I (and, increasingly, analysts at data-driven places like *FiveThirtyEight*) don't define class solely with reference to income is that class is not just about money. Nor is class an abiding characteristic of individuals. As I'll explain, it's more like a cultural tradition that people riff off as they shape their everyday behavior and make sense of their lives. And so to better understand the white working class, readers in the elite will need to understand not only the parochial folkways of the white working class. They will also need to understand their own assumptions and truths *as* parochial folkways—traditions, behaviors, and ways of life—that make no sense to the white working class, because they make no sense outside the context of elite lives.

CHAPTER 3

Why Does the Working Class Resent the Poor?

REMEMBER WHEN PRESIDENT OBAMA sold Obamacare by constantly stressing that it delivered health care to 20 million people? To many in the working class, this made it sound like just another program that taxed the middle class to help the poor. And in some cases that's proved true: the poor got health insurance, while some Americans just a tiny bit better off saw their premiums rise.[20]

Progressives have lavished attention on the poor for over a century, devising social programs targeting them. Because America is particularly testy about the kinds of taxes that many European countries take for granted, these programs are not universal. Instead, they are limited to those below a certain income level, which means they exclude those just a notch above. This is a recipe for class conflict.

Is it any wonder the working class feels "totally forgotten," to quote Annette Norris?* "I raised three children on [\$40,000 a year]. . . . But we didn't get any assistance because we did not qualify." Annette is not wrong, or alone: although about 30% of poor families using center-based child care receive subsidies, subsidies are largely nonexistent for the middle class.[21] My sister-in-law worked full time for Head Start, providing free child care for poor women while earning so little that she almost couldn't pay for her own. She resented this, especially the fact that some of the kids' moms did not work. One arrived late one day to pick up her child, carrying shopping bags from the local mall. My sister-in-law was livid.

J. D. Vance's much-heralded *Hillbilly Elegy* captures this resentment.[22] Hard-living families like that of his mother live alongside settled families like that of his biological father. While the hard-living succumb to despair, drugs, or alcohol, settled families keep to the straight and narrow, like my parents-in-law, who owned their home and sent both sons to college. To accomplish that, they lived a life of rigorous thrift and self-discipline. Vance's book passes harsh judgment on his hard-living relatives and neighbors, which is not uncommon among people from families who kept their nose clean through sheer force of will.[23]

Understanding working-class resentment of the poor needs to begin by looking at everyday life for working-class Americans of all races. Their rigid, highly supervised jobs often are boring, repetitive, or both, which makes the work psychologically challenging: think of medical technicians, factory workers, bus drivers. Men's jobs, and some women's, are physically demanding: consider construction workers, long-haul truck drivers, physicians' assistants. Women's jobs—in nursing, customer service, managing small stores—can be emotionally demanding, too.

Job demands are compounded by those of child care. Many couples tag team, with parents working different shifts to minimize child care costs. Here's what that looks like:

> *Mike drives a cab and I work in a hospital, so we figure one of us could transfer to nights. We talked it over and decided it would be best if I was here during the day and he was here at night. He controls the kids, especially my son, better than I do. So now Mike works day and I work graveyard. I hate it, but it's the only answer: at least this way somebody's here all the time. I get home at 8:30 in the morning. The kids and Mike are gone. I clean up the house a little, do the shopping and the laundry and whatever, then I go to sleep for a couple of hours before the kids get home from school. Mike gets home at 5, we eat, then he takes over for the night, and I go back to sleep for a couple of hours. I try to get up at 9:00 so we can have a little time together, but I'm so tired that I don't make it a lot of times. And by 10:00, he's sleeping because he has to get up at 6:00 in the morning. It's hard, it's very hard. There's no time to live or anything.*[24]

That's the face of working-class life today. Not easy. And it shouldn't be surprising that many—women as well as men—look back with nostalgia to their parents' generation, when women worked only intermittently or part time.

Working-class people may not know the exact statistics, but they understand the differences between their families and those of the poor. Poor married mothers (60%) are more than twice as likely to be at home full time as married mothers in the middle (23%). Nearly 60% of working-class mothers work full time; only 42% of poor moms do. In families with children in center care, 30% of poor families get subsidies; very few working-class families do (about 3%).[25]

I know, but only because I study such things, that child care subsidies for the poor are sporadic and pathetically low (sometimes $2.00 an hour).[26] I know that poor moms stay home because the minimum wage is so low they would *lose* money by working. And that poor men have trouble finding full-time work because part-time jobs allow employers to avoid paying health insurance.

Mike's family doesn't know any of that, or if they do, they may not care. All they see is their stressed-out daily lives, and they resent the subsidies and sympathy available to the poor. This resentment reflects the realities of working-class lives combined with a woeful lack of graduate-level training in policy analysis. (Joke.)

For working-class Americans, maintaining two full-time jobs and a settled life is a significant achievement, one that takes unrelenting drive and rigorous self-discipline. So when asked what traits they admire, both black and white working-class Americans mention moral traits, in contrast to elites, who derive self-worth more from merit than morality.† Working-class whites like "people who care," "who are clean," "not disruptive," "stand-up kind of people." They dislike "irresponsible people who live for the moment." The values most admired are "honesty," "being responsible," "having integrity," and "being hardworking." Those most despised are "dishonesty," "being irresponsible," and "being lazy" (see Table 1).[27]

"My father made a religion of responsibility," noted the son of a bricklayer who became a reporter; his father had "a well-developed work ethic, the kind that gets you up early and keeps you locked in until the job is done, regardless of how odious or personally distasteful the task."[28] "Sometimes I wish I could be more carefree," a printer told Michèle Lamont, the sociologist who wrote the single best book on working-class Americans. "And then I say no, I like the way I am ... I like people who are responsible."[29] Makes sense: if he were a free spirit, he might soon be homeless. So he's disciplined and looks down on "hard-living" people who aren't.

For an example of "hard living," we can look to Vance's mother. She falls into addiction and has serious impulse-control issues and a series of unsavory boyfriends. Vance was raised chiefly by his grandmother, a classic pattern in hard-living families. His father, who plays a minor role in the book and his life, represents "settled living": he owns "a

---

†Lamont's study gives percentages of the white (and black) working class who embrace the dominant values. To make the text more readable throughout this book, I have made blanket statements that actually reflect tendencies, not absolutes.

TABLE 1

Dimensions of morality most salient to white and black workers and to professionals and managers

White workers	Black workers	Professionals and managers
Hardworking[++]	Hardworking[+]	Hardworking
Responsible	Responsible	—
Providing[+]	Providing[+]	Providing
—	—	Self-actualization
Protecting	Protecting[+]	—
Personal integrity	Personal integrity	—
—	—	Flexibility/team orientation
Straightforwardness/ sincerity	Straightforwardness/ sincerity (especially in the context of racism)	—
—	—	Conflict avoidance
—	Religious participation[+]	—
Traditional morality[+] (anti-drugs and anti-crime)	Traditional morality[++] (anti-drugs and anti-crime)	Traditional morality
—	Collective solidarity	—
—	Generosity	—
Interpersonal altruism	—	—

Source: *The Dignity of Working Men: Morality and the Boundaries of Race, Class, and Immigration* by Michèle Lamont (Cambridge, MA: Harvard University Press, copyright © 2000 by the Russell Sage Foundation).

[+]Frequent

[++]Very frequent

modest house," has a stable marriage and a family life of "an almost jarring serenity." He doesn't drink and runs a highly religious family with strict rules of behavior. Vance didn't want to live with him, because Led Zeppelin was not accepted. Vance escaped his mother's hard-living life by joining the military, which gave him what his upbringing failed to provide. For kids from hard-living families, the military provides a reset button—a proxy for being brought up in a stable and ordered environment.[30]

A study of California's Central Valley found that in settled-living families, typically both parents are high school graduates, with at least one stable job between them and health insurance.[31] They maintain strict control over their children and expect them to finish high school,[32] keep their nose clean, and not run wild. The working class values responsibility "because they are highly dependent on the actions of others.... The physical conditions in which they work and live and their limited financial resources make it difficult for them to buffer themselves from the actions of neighbors, coworkers, kin, and friends," notes Lamont.[33] A friend from Atlanta remarks, "Why did people vote for Trump? All they want is a three-bedroom, two-bath cinderblock house. But now they're losing those homes." The working class worries that opportunities for a settled life are slipping away.

Maria Kefalas's study of working-class Chicago described houses set very close together, with "elaborate lawn decorations, manicured grass, color-coordinated kitchens, [and] American-made cars."[34] And owners house-proud and insistent on upkeep; "[m]uch more is at stake than dust bunnies."[35] Well-kept homes are "an outward manifestation of work ethics,"[36] notes Jennifer Sherman's study of a rural community in California.

The professional elite also values hard work, of course— but it's different. To working-class members of all races, valuing hard work means having the rigid self-discipline to do a menial job you hate for 40 years, and reining yourself in so you don't "have an attitude" (i.e., so that you can submit to authority). Hard work for elites is associated with self-actualization; "disruption" means founding a successful start-up. Disruption, in working-class jobs, just gets you fired.

Free spirits born working class can't count on the second chances available to elites. That's why blue-collar families are so big on stability and self-discipline, and they embrace institutions that support these traits. Chief among these is religion. The devout have greater impulse control and "tend to do better in school, live longer, have more satisfying marriages and be generally happier."[37] "Regular church attendees commit fewer crimes, are in better health, live longer, make more money, drop out of high school less frequently, and finish college more frequently than those who don't attend church at all."[38] Churchgoing can also provide a financial safety net: when Vance's father had financial troubles, people in his church bought him a used car so he could get back on his feet.[39]

And going to church regularly is not just correlated with good actions; it seems to prompt people to be their best selves.[40] One class migrant recalled her struggles in high school: "Learnedness itself was suspect, and making a display of learning was simply not done; in school as elsewhere, the worst failure of character was to get a 'swelled head.' You could do intellectual work, though, if you called it something else. We called it religion."[41] For many in the working class, churches provide the kind of mental exercise, stability, hopefulness, future orientation, impulse control, and social safety net many in the professional elite get from their families, their career potential, their therapists, and their bank accounts.

Tea Party members believe the "federal government was taking money from … people of good character and giving to people of bad character,"[42] found a 2016 study. Researchers have found the same belief time and again. Means-tested programs inadvertently set the "have-a-littles" against the "have-nots," noted an Italian lawyer interviewed by Jonathan Rieder in his 1985 book.[43] In his high school job at a grocery, Vance "learned how people gamed the welfare system." They'd buy sodas with food stamps and then sell them, or use food stamps for food and their own money for beer, wine, and cigarettes. He'd see them going through the checkout lines using cell phones. How could they afford cell phones? "I could never understand why our lives felt like a struggle," wrote Vance of his own family, "while those living off of government largesse enjoyed trinkets that I only dreamed about."[44]

Government benefits tied to work are seen quite differently. Unemployment is seen "as income that a person deserves and has basically worked for." Disability is seen as symbolizing past hard, dangerous work. In sharp contrast, means-tested benefits were stigmatized. In rural California, Sherman found that food stamps and TANF (Temporary Assistance for Needy Families) triggered "strong social disgrace." One family drove an hour or more from home to use their food stamps when the husband was unemployed. "I don't want to be considered lazy or a freeloader or something like that," the wife explained. "You want people to think you're a hard worker—and, you know, we pride ourselves on that," she added. The stigma associated with welfare and food stamps has concrete economic consequences. In the community Sherman studied, only those in good moral standing were considered for the few cherished job openings. Those without good moral standing also jeopardized their access to community-level charity.[45]

I spoke with Lisa McCorkell, who worked as a financial counselor, who told me, "When I spoke with working-class people across the country about their financial issues, whether it be crippling debt, impending foreclosure, unemployment, or all three, I found that they were much more likely than the poor to reject the government benefits they were eligible for, at least until it was absolutely necessary to survive. They saw it as an affront to their dignity. I heard so often things like, 'I don't want a government handout; I can do this on my own.' So even when they were aware of the government benefits they were entitled to, they did not accept them."

When it comes to attitudes toward government programs, working-class African-Americans differ from whites in an important way: African-Americans understand the structural nature of inequality. Working-class African-Americans are more like the French (and unlike white working-class Americans) in their nonjudgmental "there but for the grace of God go I" attitude toward the poor, and their felt need for solidarity.[46]

All this explains why Bill Clinton, the last Democratic president to truly understand the white working class, ended "welfare as we know it." He understood it was political poison to allow poor women to remain stay-at-home moms while Mike's family tag-teamed its way to exhaustion. What went deeply wrong was that the replacement TANF program failed to provide the kind of support necessary for working families. By 2006, in poor familes, 7.5% of children aged 5–8 were home alone; nearly 14% of kids 9–11 were.[47]

If America's policymakers better understood white working-class anger against the social safety net, they might have a shot at creating programs that don't get gutted in this way. Far from abandoning the poor, we'd be doing a better job of helping them.

CHAPTER 4

Why Does the Working Class Resent Professionals but Admire the Rich?

MEMBERS OF THE ELITE tend to assume that working-class people want to join their ranks. This is not always true.

Professionals aren't necessarily admired. Many are seen as suspect. Managers are seen as college kids "who don't know shit about how to do anything, but are full of ideas about how I have to do my job."[48] Barbara Ehrenreich recalled in 1990 that her blue-collar dad "could not say the word *doctor* without the virtual prefix *quack*. Lawyers were *shysters* ... and professors were without exception *phonies*."[49] Sociologist Annette Lareau also found mistrust of doctors and other health professionals. She also found resentment against teachers by working-class parents, who perceived their children's educators as condescending and unhelpful[50]—a resentment that perhaps fuels working-class support for conservatives' assault on teachers' unions.[51]

However, this resentment of professionals does not extend to the rich. "There's an almost mystical desire among the working class to see a rich person from the upper class reach out to them," commented class migrant Eric Sansoni* (remember, a class migrant is someone who starts in one class but moves to another—in this case, out of the working class and into a professional job). "[I] can't knock anyone for succeeding," a laborer told Lamont. "There's a lot of people out there who are wealthy and I'm sure they worked darned hard for every cent they have," chimed in a receiving clerk.[52] "The main thing is to be independent and give your own orders and not have to take them from anybody else," said a machine operator. The ideal is to own a business. "The dream of self-employment is one *expression* of class consciousness, not a denial of it," noted an influential book on class.[53]

Daily life reinforces admiration of the rich but resentment of professionals. Most working-class people have little contact with the truly rich outside of "The Apprentice" or "Lifestyles of the Rich and Famous," but they suffer class affronts from professionals every day: the doctor who unthinkingly patronizes the medical technician, the harried office worker who treats the security guard as invisible, the overbooked business traveler who snaps at the TSA agent.

Remember: class isn't just about money. Everything we do is class-marked. Especially today. Although my family was wealthy, my mom shopped at Sears and the A&P, I went to

public school, and everyone watched the evening news with
Walter Cronkite. Today, the professional elite sends their kids
to private schools, shops at Whole Foods, and reads *Slate* instead of watching Fox. Floods of ink cover the increased segmentation of the American media market, but almost no one
makes the obvious point that the segmentation is shaped by
social class. My circle of friends would no more send a Hall-
mark card than eat at TGI Friday's. We all know what's classy,
though we wouldn't be so gauche as to admit it.

Or consider coffee, a daily part of most Americans' lives.
When I was growing up in the 1960s, there were two kinds
of coffee: decent and burnt. But over the past 30 years, a class
structure of coffee has emerged. In the Rust Belt city where
my in-laws live, you still go to Dunkin' Donuts for a good
cup. Not where I live in San Francisco: it's all local coffee
shops, with pour-overs starting at $6 a cup. And what of Star-
bucks? As Starbucks has democratized, and its drinks made
sweeter and fattier, my PME friends wouldn't think of setting foot in a Starbucks. Seeking to recapture that market, the
ubiquitous chain recently announced a new premium coffee
for $12 a cup.[54]

Not only the mundane is class-marked. So is the sublime.
Among the elite, we proudly announce we are "spiritual
but not religious" and invent some unique blend. Developing one's own personal mélange of world religions reflects
our taste for novelty and our penchant for self-development.
Conventional religion? So down market.

Looking down on religion is a commonplace form of modern snobbery. I think it's silly. Personally, I don't believe in

God but I do believe in religion. Religion helps me sit quietly, listening to beautiful music, among a group of people trying to be their best selves. I'm offended by the likes of Richard Dawkins—so dismissive of sincerely held beliefs.[55] Some believe God exists, while others see religion as a metaphorical structure that gives shape to their deepest aspirations and griefs. Ontological questions don't interest me.

Why do elites seek out novelty while the working class seeks out stability? For one thing, elites can afford it—star fruit costs more than bananas—but there's more to it than that. The elite gains social honor by displaying their sophistication; the white working class has different fish to fry.

The contrast is most vivid at dinner parties. Anthropologist Arlie Hochschild, for her book *Strangers in Their Own Land,* traveled to Louisiana where she interviewed and got to know locals who identified as members of the Tea Party. For Hochschild's Tea Party friends, a good party typically consisted of extended family getting together for "steaming roast beef, gravy, potatoes, okra, green beans, corn bread, and sweetened ice tea"[56]—large portions of familiar favorites and familiar faces, signaling comforting stability. For my crowd, a good party means a day of intensive cooking, often not for people we know well already, but for "people we'd like to know better." What's on display? Novelty is meant to signal sophistication; cultural capital, sociologists would call it. It's important to impress, all the more so because the dinner party often serves a work purpose as well as a social one; it's designed to cement relationships that will be helpful in developing a career—colleagues or potential clients or customers.

If food and religion are deep class divides, so is the role of talk. Elite families talk with their children far more than non-elite ones do.[57] "While working-class people are not without self-insight and concern about their inward states, nevertheless they are not typically occupied with their 'innards' on the scale of the middle class," noted a class migrant, now a professor.[58] J. D. Vance tried going to a therapist but "talking with some stranger about my feelings made me want to vomit."[59] This response also reflects the high value placed on privacy, on not "spilling your guts." Noted one class migrant who grew up in North Dakota, "In my family, a conversation about one's work typically consumed only six words. ('How was your day?' 'Oh, fine.') Speaking otherwise, in detail or with enthusiasm, was to risk display of the dreaded swelled head."[60] So much for discussing that amazing book you're reading.

Still another class divide concerns social networks.[61] Elites typically have a narrow intimate circle but also have a broad network of acquaintances—"entrepreneurial networks," sociologists call them. Entrepreneurial networks help professionals get jobs, customers, clients, business partners, and business opportunities around the country or even in other countries.

Elite socializing thus cultivates the ability to get along smoothly with a broad range of people and impress them with your sophistication. Elite children are taught from a very young age to shake hands and look strangers firmly in the eye, [62] because their futures rely on the ability to form and maintain entrepreneurial networks. Studies show that between 51% and 70% of professionals get jobs through personal contacts, so they "network" and host those aforementioned dinner parties.[63] This is part of the self-actualization ethic so central to elite life (see Table 1).

This peculiar combination of the personal and the strategic strikes the working class as insincere. So does the kind of politicking required for career success in professional and business careers. Working-class entertaining is designed to denote a space *apart* from jobs, not be an extension of them. The goal is not to impress people you don't know well, but to comfort those you do with abundant portions of familiar dishes—think Old Country Buffet, not Chez Panisse.

Blue-collar jobs often involve technical rather than social skills, and the working class takes pride in their technical expertise, not their ability to influence other people. A pipe fitter criticized "shirt and ties types" for "too much politicking." "They are jockeying for jobs and worrying about whether they are making the right moves and stuff. I feel that I don't have to get involved in that." Working-class men often see professionals as phony and value their own ability to call a spade a spade. Said a man who had left Wall Street to be a firefighter, "In big business, there's a lot of false stuff going on." Said an auto mechanic, "You know what I hate? Two-face. I can't stand that. You're a fake, you're a fake. Why be a fake?"[64] "Middle-class game-playing bullshit" was the verdict of one class migrant.[65]

Irony versus sincerity is yet another class divide. Both black and white workers value sincerity and direct talk because they believe it sets them above the (fake, suck-up) professionals. The professional elite values irony and polish, because this sets them above the (inarticulate, unsophisticated) working class.

So much of what the professional elite identifies as normal life the white working class sees as the display of class privilege. Take the standard professional-class ice-breaker: "What do you do?" It makes sense in a class context where personal dignity stems from economic power and professional achievement. When people ask me, I reply, "I'm a law professor."

But that kind of honor is available to only a few in the working class—to firefighters, police, soldiers. For most, the dignity work affords is from what it allows you to buy and whom it allows you to support, not from the job itself. "What do you do?" is not the first question at a party. I remember attending my class-migrant husband's high school reunion when, with a regrettable lack of code switching, he posed the "What do you do?" question to a classmate. The classmate's face got very red as he came right up into Jim's face and hissed, "I sell *toilets*."

This helps explain why, in working-class communities, attention often shifts from *what one does* to *who one is*—to character. Working-class whites seek to "keep the world in moral order," to quote Lamont, often measured by adherence to "traditional" values.[66] "I was seldom entirely clear about what was meant by tradition," admits Sherman, but the rural whites she interviewed were all for it. For them, it meant both rural rootedness and family values, which meant the two-parent family, the stability of family life, and the high value placed on family caregiving.[67]

For people whose jobs deny them prestige, "family comes first" is a common refrain. As a retired mill worker told Sherman, in his life everything was built around family. Having a "successful nuclear family was one of his life's greatest achievements," notes Sherman. Connecting to tradition through aspirational family structure allows working-class whites "to claim moral and personal success when they have few other opportunities to achieve some version of the American dream," she concludes.[68] This is why family values are so resonant.

The high value placed on traditional family values creates another clash with the professional class: among elites, a key way they show sophistication is to signal comfort with avant-garde sexuality, self-presentation, and family dynamics. The avant-garde arose in the early nineteenth century as an artistic movement that "pushes the boundaries of what is accepted as the norm or the status quo, primarily in the cultural realm."[69] What began as transgression among nineteenth-century European artists now defines the cultural world of the twenty-first-century American elite: it's a point of pride not to be one of those petty bourgeois who's shocked by sexual transgression. I knew I was born to live in San Francisco when, driving down Market Street, I spotted a man sporting sturdy shoes—and nothing else. I was uncomfortable—and delighted.

Securing approval for a new range of sexualities is a cause now embraced by progressives and mainstream conservatives alike (as evidenced by the partnership of Ted Olson and David Boies in arguing a landmark marriage equality case).

Ted Olson's championship of marriage equality in the Supreme Court dramatized that mainstream conservatives have joined the progressive elite in embracing acceptance of formerly transgressive sexualities as being open-minded and sophisticated rather than narrow and provincial.

The professional class seeks social honor by embracing the edgy; the white working class seeks social honor by embracing the traditional. The focus on character, morality, and family values is a key expression of class disadvantage; we all choose baskets we can fill. This attachment to tradition is part of what the white working class shared for so long with Burkean conservatives.[70]

All this is crucial background to understanding why working-class whites resent professionals. The professional-class values of sophistication, boundary breaking, and creativity are all useful for getting and keeping a job if you're an order giver who has to signal initiative. Working-class whites value stability and dependability—dispositions useful for getting and keeping a job if you're an order taker.[71]

For many in the working class, becoming a member of the professional class is an ambiguous achievement—you have more money, yes, but you also have to adopt new folkways, like two-facedness. The dream is to live in your own class milieu, where you feel comfortable—just with more money.[72] Brashly wealthy celebrities epitomize the fantasy of being wildly rich while losing none of your working-class cred. Trump epitomizes this—after all, his original fortune was made in garish casinos that sold a working-class brand of luxury (aka "garish bad taste").[73]

Bridging the class culture gap is difficult—for professionals as well as the working class. The first step is to recognize elite folkways as just that: folkways, not "good taste." Many habits of the professional elite—from artisanal religion to a life of self-actualization—require a college education. America doesn't provide that, so we need to take the working class as we find them. We don't fault the poor for failing to value the same things the professional class values. We need to extend that courtesy to working-class people of all races. Many of our truths just don't make sense in the context of their lives.

CHAPTER 5

Why Doesn't the Working Class Just Move to Where the Jobs Are?

ONE BIG QUESTION pundits and commentators mull over is this: why don't people facing hard economic times move to where economic times are better? If you live in Detroit, Michigan; Millinocket, Maine; Camden, New Jersey; York, Pennsylvania; or Yuma, Arizona,[74] why not move to an area where the economy is growing? At best, elites are puzzled. At worst, they're patronizing and even scornful. "Donald Trump cannot deliver new jobs like pizza wherever you live," said Glenn Helton,* decrying the "stubborn immobility of the white working class."

Part of the reason is the power of "clique networks," as sociologists call them, where everybody knows everyone else and ties run deep.[75] This has a practical side to it: in the working class of all races, family ties also involve material help with child care and home improvements—things wealthier families buy. Clique networks help protect working-class families from their vulnerable market position.

The folkways of elites are very different. Professionals' national job markets also mean they often end up far away from their families, and family relationships among adults typically involve purely emotional ties: families support one another by talking things through. If working-class networks are narrow and deep, professionals' are broad but shallow.

A class-migrant professor tried to explain to a colleague why he saw his distant family so much more than his colleague saw his (who lived closer): "It's a blue-collar thing.... Middle-class kids are groomed to fly away, and they do. The working class likes to keep its young close to home."[76] Tearing a working-class person from the network that defines their life is a far heavier lift than insisting that a Harvard grad move to Silicon Valley.

The professional elite values change and self-development; working-class families value stability and community. The professional elite associates change with challenge, excitement, opportunity, and innovation. But for families a few paychecks away from losing their homes and stable middle-class lives, respect for stability reigns supreme. "I associate change with loss," said a class migrant whose father was evicted from apartment after apartment. Moving to a new city or state is often appealing for someone from the professional elite, and an alarming prospect for someone from the working class. (By the way, the working class shares this with low-income Americans of all races, who also tend to stay close to home, for many of the same reasons.)

Moving for a job doesn't strike the professional elite as a big deal, because the professional elite relies heavily on work to shape identity. A study of health professionals in Massachusetts found doctors' lives shaped by what sociologist Mary Blair-Loy calls the "work devotion schema": high-level professionals are expected to "maintain a single-minded focus" on work in which "[a]ny nonwork activities pale ... in significance ... [to] professional responsibilities." This ideal has its roots in the Protestant work ethic, in which work was viewed as a "calling" from God.[77]

For many in the professional elite, work becomes a totalizing experience. "Holidays are a nuisance because you have to stop working," said a corporate litigator. "I remember being really annoyed when it was Thanksgiving. Damn, why did I have to stop working to go eat a turkey? I missed my favorite uncle's funeral, because I had a deposition scheduled that was too important."[78]

Working-class men find this obsession with work off-putting. Thus a salesman decried overly ambitious people who "have blinders on. You miss all of life.... A person that is totally ambitious and driven never sees anything except the spot they are aiming at." Working-class men dismiss work devotion as narcissism. An electronics technician criticized people who are "so self-assured, so self-intense that they don't really care about anyone else.... It's me, me, me, me, me. I'm not that kind of person at all, and that's probably why I don't like it."[79]

But elite men embrace work devotion as integral to manliness. Working long hours is seen as a "heroic activity," noted a study of lawyers.[80] For Silicon Valley engineers, working long hours turns computer keyboarding into a manly test of physical endurance. "There's this kind of machismo culture among young male engineers that you just don't sleep," one engineer told Marianne Cooper.[81] "[S]uccessful enactment of this masculinity," she concludes, "involves displaying one's exhaustion, physically and verbally, in order to convey the depth of one's commitment, stamina, and virility."[82]

For elite men, ambition and a strong work ethic are "doubly sacred ... [as signals of] both moral and socioeconomic worth."[83] Work, in some sense, *is* their religion. Recognizing that may make us less condescending about Americans who worship a different God and arguably have a healthier relationship to work.

Moving for a job makes sense in this context, if you know a million former college classmates in Chicago anyway. But moving means something very different for working-class people. Remember the fellow who hissed, "I sell toilets"? It's safer to hang out with people you've known forever who will not judge you on your often-inglorious job. Familiar faces provide a buffer against humiliation.

Then there's the question of what moving away might imply: that you care more about your job than your community. Part of the reason the working class doesn't move to where the jobs are is because of these deep ties to their communities. And this communitarian streak manifests in other, clearly laudable ways. Households earning $50,000 to $75,000 give away far more of their discretionary income (7.6%) than do households earning $100,000 or more (4.2%).[84] The middle-class Maryland towns of Capitol Heights (majority white) and Suitland[85] (majority black) give away a higher proportion of their incomes than the tony suburbs of McLean, Virginia, and Bethesda, Maryland.[86] Remember how Vance's father's church bought him a car when he was unemployed? These were not affluent people.

Sherman describes a white rural family that sheltered and fed, over the years, some 200 local kids who were escaping physical abuse or parental addiction. This was a serious financial strain, but nearly half of the 55 people Sherman interviewed had cared for children who were not biologically related to them.[87]

Non-privileged people, whether poor or working class, tend to be more rooted than American elites. Their lack of market power means that they rely on close networks of family and friends for many things more affluent folks purchase on the open market, from child and elder care to home improvement projects. Moving would eliminate this safety net, and having to pay for child care might well erase the economic benefits of moving.

At a deeper level, non-privileged people invest much more of their identities in their close-knit families and communities than do more privileged ones. Poor and working-class people derive social honor from their reputations in communities of people who've known them "forever." Moving for them is not like moving from New York to San Francisco to crash in your college roommate's apartment while you found a start-up among people who have been trained since childhood to build fluid careers based on fluid networks of personal and business acquaintances. It's throwing away the only relationships that give you the prospect of social honor, the only social life you know how to create, and the social safety net that has seen you through.

Among the poor and the working class, social lives often revolve around family. This begins early: Annette Lareau notes that children often play with cousins and that "it would be hard to overstate the importance of family" in white working-class lives.[88] For decades, my sister-in-law went grocery shopping every weekend with her mother, which I thought was bizarre until I decided it was brilliant. Now I go to Costco every weekend with my son, but I don't know anyone else who does anything like that. A man described to Hochschild that he "had grown up in a dense circle of aunts, uncles, cousins, and grandparents all within walking distance of each other."[89] Again, there are material reasons that make it harder for working-class people to just pull up roots and move.

Blue-state families are better off than red-state ones, who have higher rates of teenage pregnancy and lower ages of marriage and first birth,[90] as progressives delight in pointing out as an example of hypocrisy. But that's not the point. Family values are about *aspiration*. Until about 1980, young adults in the working class were like college grads: they waited to have children until they were married. But now Americans who are not college grads don't wait.[91] Instead they behave more like the poor, who have been having children out of wedlock for quite a while.[92]

Why? Americans tend to associate marriage with the white picket fence—a stable job, stable home, stable life. If you feel that stability is attainable, you wait until you have it before marriage and kids. But if Americans feel that's not a practical goal, or only an extremely long-term and aspirational one, they tend not to marry. The decline in marriage is a *symptom* of the working class's economic decline—not, as some argue, its cause.[93]

The rootlessness of the PME makes sense in their lives: they have friends and classmates throughout the country or the world, their job markets are national or global, their family ties are chiefly emotional rather than practical or economic—and when someone in the professional class moves, they can maintain those emotional ties through unlimited international data plans.[94] But both the poor and the working class of all races typically are deeply rooted, both by disposition and necessity. You can't provide child care for your grandchildren via Skype.

CHAPTER 6

Why Doesn't the Working Class Get with It and Go to College?

EDUCATIONAL LEVELS DO NOT just reflect social class, they are *constitutive* of it. Graduating from college is a class act that both enacts class status and reproduces it.

Pierre Bourdieu, whose name is associated with the idea that class is expressed through cultural differences, urges us to pay attention to the taken-for-granted assumptions different groups use to create their reality.[95] Higher education is a perfect example: in elite families, it's simply unthinkable not to go to college (no matter how much debt you have to take on to do it). A common sentiment among the white working class is that college is optional—and sometimes, undesirable.

Michael Long* expressed it this way: "You don't need a college degree, you need to have a skill that people will pay you for. It's as simple as that.... [S]ometimes the poor decision is going to college." That is a common working-class attitude. A typical elite response comes from a software engineer: "My seemingly cutting-edge job [is] only as secure as I made it for myself ... why in God's name am I supposed to feel sympathy for people whose laziness and sense of entitlement runs so deep that they are pining for jobs that were already gone before they were born?"

"And they refuse any other work except the jobs that have been lost to advances in technology and trade? The kind of jobs that are NEVER coming back?" commented Amanda Fernandez.* "I feel terrible about your father-in-law but for some reason, he did not pursue a path out of his plight," Rachel Corbett wrote me. "Why did he not pursue education or learn a trade? So that he could work at a job he may have liked? ... If the white working class's lot in life is so bad, why don't they do something? Go to school."

As blue-collar jobs disappeared and communities withered in rural areas and Rust Belt cities, we have not responded with good jobs for "school leavers" (as the British call them). That phrase says it all: if you want a good living, get a college education and a white-collar future. If you leave school, you get what you deserve.

On the right, the talk is of bootstraps and college loans. On the left, it's of Pell grants and affordable tuitions. But the prescription is the same: a college degree. This ignores an important fact: only 33% of Americans obtain college degrees.[96] *Two-thirds of Americans do not have college degrees.* I'm always surprised by how few people in the PME know this fact.

The working class is not flocking to college. In the past three decades, college graduates' earnings have climbed to 60% higher than those of high school graduates, but the proportion of Americans who completed four-year degrees has not risen substantially. A slight increase in the percentage of women who graduate was offset by a decrease in the percentage of men.[97]

Insistence on college makes sense for professional elite kids: for them, it's the prerequisite that allows them to reproduce their parents' class status. But college may not make economic sense for working-class kids. It's a much riskier decision that may not pay off. Working-class kids worry they might end up with a first-class degree and still fail to get a job because they don't know the unwritten social codes of professional life; a British news report told of class migrants failing to get investment banking jobs in London because they didn't know the "no brown in town" rule (i.e., don't wear brown shoes in the City).[98] Vance relied on his professional-class girlfriend to explain the folkways of her class. Without her, he notes, he lacked the social capital to navigate an elite career. At an interview, he called her from the restroom to find out which fork to use. Lucky he did: "the[se] interviews were about passing a social test—a test of belonging, of holding your own in a corporate boardroom, of making connections with potential future clients."[99]

Research by Lauren Rivera and András Tilcsik put some numbers behind this when they sent over 300 fictitious resumes to 147 top law firms. "All applicants were in the top 1% of their class and were on law review," and they had identical (and impressive) work and academic achievements, they write. The researchers also inserted subtle cues about social class "via accepted and often required portions of resumes: awards and extracurricular activities." For example, the lower-class applicant was listed as enjoying pick-up soccer and country music and volunteered as a mentor for fellow first-generation college students, while the upper-class applicant enjoyed sailing and classical music and volunteered as a generic student mentor.

The employers overwhelmingly favored the higher-class man: over 16% of his resumes resulted in a callback. Only about 1% of the lower-class man's resumes did so, even though he was just as qualified.[100] What's the payoff on his education?

Americans assume college is a class escalator, and it can be for the nonelite kids who make it into Yale or Harvard. But few do. A recent study found that 38 colleges, including five in the Ivy League, have more students from the top 1% than from the entire bottom 60% of the income distribution. Far less than 10% of college students in the middle three quintiles of family income go to very selective schools, and less than 3% go to elites or Ivys.[101]

The American higher education system operates as a "caste system: it takes Americans who grew up in different social strata and it widens the divisions between them," concludes public policy expert Suzanne Mettler.[102] It's easier for elite kids to get into selective schools because parents' social networks give them access to the people who matter and because elite kids can do the unpaid internships and community service selective colleges now expect to see on their applications. It's also just easier to get in, period. A child from the professional elite is three times more likely to be admitted to a selective private institution than a lower-class white with similar qualifications.[103]

At a more basic level, working-class kids not only may not know how to get into elite schools; often they don't even understand that there's a big difference between going to Amherst and Michigan State. Indeed, they may have never heard of Amherst. One class migrant who ended up attending Brown wrote that her guidance counselor didn't have much guidance to give: "He didn't know much about Brown or any other schools I was applying to, didn't have any advice for applying, and didn't look into it afterwards." Her younger sister, who ended up at Wellesley, fared little better: her counselor didn't even know where Wellesley was. She also remembers that their counselors would sometimes actively discourage them and their friends from applying to top-tier schools. The attitude was "You'll never get in, that's not for you, why'd you want to go there?" remembers their cousin.

Part of this is geographical. Kids are more likely to hear about a college that is close by, and fully 57% of selective colleges are in the Northeast or California.[104] So-called education deserts, or communities in which there are either zero colleges or universities, or only one community college nearby, are mostly situated in the rural areas of the Midwest and Great Plains, where many white working-class kids live. In contrast, professional-class kids often go to colleges far from home. Their families miss them, but typically feel it would be inappropriate to complain. Not so with working-class families, who expect their kids to remain in their families' clique network throughout their lives. (This is particularly true of Latinos, but also holds for many whites.)[105]

Even if they've heard about selective schools, working-class kids of all races also know they're expensive. They may not know scholarships are available, or may be unable to pay even application fees.

And like poor kids, working-class kids may be less likely to have the kind of school records that make them eligible for admission at selective schools. In the professional elite, learning disabilities typically lead to intensive tutoring and private school; in overcrowded public schools, similar kids may be treated as just average if they are well behaved, or downright disruptive if they disinvest in school. Many working-class parents can't help with homework, because their work schedules take them away from home in the evenings. They may not know the difference between college-prep and non-college-prep courses; they may not know much of anything about college entrance exams either.

Working-class college students who do go to college typically go to schools close to home with modest reputations. Though attending those schools may cost less than a selective school that is farther away (studying close to home allows students to save on transportation and living expenses),[106] the return on investment is not clear cut. Wage inequality has increased among college graduates. Today, a top-earning male college graduate earns 90% more than a low-earning one; in 1979, that figure was 60% for women and 70% for men. One reason for the decreased returns to some with college degrees is that an increasing number of male college grads end up in low- or medium-skilled jobs. And a significant proportion of both male (19.4%) and female (14.0%) college grads earn *less* than does the average high-school graduate.[107]

And then there's the debt. "I still value education," wrote Diana Johnson,* "although it has gotten me nowhere, and in much debt." Average college debt among graduating seniors who had taken out student loans more than doubled between 1986 and 2008,[108] and increased 56% in the decade before 2014.[109] In the 30 years since 1980, "the inflation-adjusted cost of college tuition and fees rose as much or more than the returns to a college education."[110] Taking on this amount of debt is a risky business for a kid from a working-class family. Students who don't complete their degrees may end up worse off than if they'd never started: with a lot of debt, and no extra earning power. In 2009, student loans were siphoning off 35% of college dropouts' annual income.[111]

Another reason many working-class kids don't go to college is that they don't want to be "pencil pushers."[112] "A great many people in agriculture, from the person driving the tractor or loading feed at the co-op all the way to allied industry executives, honestly take pride in the fact they are feeding the world. Don't laugh at this," wrote Cathy Bandyk.* Oil workers are proud they keep the economy going.[113] Others want to work with their hands or believe that being a firefighter adds greater value to the community than designing ever-more-attention-grabbing Google ads.

And then there's that uncomfortable fact that some aren't suited to intellectual work. "The mantra on more college, more college ... is a good theory, but could everyone learn in the higher spectrum of knowledge? And if you cannot learn to be 'smart' but possess a strong back and a strong work ethic ... [s]hould that be diminished to tiny wages with no benefits although the occupation be a societal necessity? ... I was raised to respect all working people and so I continue and muddle on," commented Leo Baranovsky.*

So there are lots of reasons why college, which is such a no-brainer investment for professional-class kids, may not be as good or as safe an investment for working-class kids. They're not ignorant and lazy. They just live in a different world.

Moreover, those who try to move from a familiar world to a new one often uncomfortably end up with one foot in each. The class culture gap can create uncomfortable rifts between class migrants and their families. "My dad was a taxi driver," an Irish professional wrote me. "After every degree, he would say, half joking but wholly in earnest, 'what can you do now?' When I got my first PhD and could teach, he stopped asking. I know he was happy for me, but fundamentally he was pretty sure these professional jobs were bullshit jobs. 15 years later I'm more on his side than I thought."

When a Harvard-educated lawyer went into public interest law, his working-class parents found his career path mysterious. "What did they expect?" I asked. "Isn't this what they wanted?" Nope: "What they wanted was for me to stay in [the Rust Belt city where he grew up] and buy a big car and a big house. Sort of like the real estate agent my mom worked for." What they wanted was to keep him home, in body and mind—just with more money. That's not what they got.[114]

Incomprehension may bleed into hostility. "That's the education talking," class migrants often hear. "I feel like I have changed sides in some very important game," noted one.[115] Lamont mentions the disapproval of "people who forget where they come from."[116] "Admitting to ability or intelligence was a great sin and indicated that you were 'stuck on yourself,'" noted another class migrant. She worked in her hometown as a carhop to make money for college and went to great pains to fit in. She thought she'd succeeded when the handsomest boy around asked her out. But then he stood her up, and she gradually realized the whole thing had been deliberately planned. "Perhaps in their view, it was retribution because they were somehow being stood up by me. I was deserting my class; they knew their place."[117]

Finally, there are the insults working-class students experience in the classroom. "[M]any of the professors resented having to teach us. One of them once described in class the mission of the school as 'teaching the first generation of immigrant children how to eat with a knife and fork,'" said a class migrant from an immigrant background.[118] Professors typically attended elite institutions, and some feel deflated and resentful when they end up teaching working-class kids at lower-ranked schools. Professors who would never let a racist comment pass their lips openly embrace "the stereotype of the southern redneck as racist, sexist, alcoholic, ignorant, and lazy.... redneck jokes may be the last acceptable ethnic slurs in 'polite' society," reports a Southern class migrant.[119] "A lot of my friends who did not make it to college were those who would not stand for that kind of treatment; they insulted back," noted another class migrant.[120] Yet another reason working-class kids don't go to college or finish it.

Socially, working-class students can also be ostracized. It's not unusual for college parties to have a "white trash" or "trailer trash" theme, even as themes that stigmatize other groups have been banned. How welcome would you feel at a party in which you and your family were unselfconsciously called garbage?

CHAPTER 7

Why Don't They
Push Their Kids
Harder to Succeed?

CHILDREN LEARN CLASS at their mothers' knee. Child-rearing, like so many other aspects of daily life, is demarcated by class. Working-class and low-income families follow what Annette Lareau, in her important book *Unequal Childhoods*, called the "accomplishment of natural growth." They view "children's development as unfolding spontaneously, as long as they [are] provided with comfort, food, shelter" and other basics. Providing these represents a challenge and is held to be a considerable achievement.[121]

Clear boundaries exist between parents and children, with prompt obedience expected: crucial training for working-class jobs.[122] Class migrants often note with shock the disrespectful way professional elite children talk of and to their parents. Noted bell hooks, whose father worked for 30 years as a janitor, "we were taught to value our parents and their care, to understand that they were not obligated to give us care."[123]

The ideology of natural growth prevalent among the poor and the working class contrasts with the "concerted cultivation" of the professional elite. "[T]he older children's schedules set the pace of life for all family members," notes Lareau, and that pace was intense. Elite children do far more organized activities (4.6 for white children, 5.2 for black children) than do nonelite kids (2.3 and 2.8, respectively).[124] Elite kids' Taylorized[125] leisure time helps them develop the skills required for white-collar jobs: how to "set priorities, manage an itinerary, shake hands with strangers, and work on a team," "work smoothly with acquaintances," and handle both victory and defeat "in a gracious way."[126] Everything is scheduled by adults, and the schedule is intense: "Tomorrow is really nuts. We have a soccer game, then a baseball game, then another soccer game," said one dad. Unlike in nonelite families, children of the elite are taught not to prioritize family: Lareau describes a child who decides to skip an important family gathering because soccer is "more of a priority."[127]

Concerted cultivation is the rehearsal for a life of work devotion: the time pressure, the intense competition, the exhaustion with it all, the ethic of putting work before family. The pressure-cooker environment in elite homes often strikes the working class as off. "I just kept thinking these kids don't know how to play," said a class migrant from a self-described "hillbilly" family.[128] "I think he doesn't enjoy doing what he's doing half the time [light laughter]," one woman told sociologist Annette Lareau. Others acknowledged that the busy schedules might pay off "job-wise" but expressed serious reservations: "I think he is a sad kid"; "He must be dead-dog tired."[129]

Elite college admissions officers agree. A group convened at Harvard asked admissions officers to allow space on applications for no more than four extracurricular activities, and "applications should state plainly that students should feel no pressure to report more than two or three substantive extracurricular activities."[130] Pretty weak sauce, but evidence that performance pressure on elite kids has gotten out of hand.

The all-consuming nature of elite parenting—typically synonymous with "elite mothering"—comes back to bite women of the professional class, and not just in the form of exhaustion. Remember the study of elite law firms in the previous chapter? The one that found elite men are vastly more preferred for jobs than nonelite men? The same study found that the reverse is true for women. While the female job applicants in their study didn't get nearly as many callbacks as the elite men, the nonelite women got *more* callbacks than the elite women. Class privilege helps men at work; it seems to hold women back. Why? Because elite women are seen as a "flight risk," people who will opt out of work to engage in the all-or-nothing elite battle to get their kids into a top college, to start the cycle of competition and achievement over again.[131]

Concerted cultivation is a strikingly recent phenomenon. Both my mother (b. 1918) and my mother-in-law

(b. 1923)—one affluent, one working class—thought my generation was truly crazy. My childhood is captured by the wonderful Mrs. Piggle-Wiggle books published in the late 1940s and 1950s. These charming books tell the story of Mrs. Piggle-Wiggle, an expert at curing children's misbehavior. Mothers focus their attention on adult things while kids engage in unstructured play. No mother is ever depicted playing with her children. Nor do children expect to be entertained; they do an endless stream of errands and chores for adults and are sent outside to entertain themselves. Only one, a spoiled rich kid, has any organized activities: a piano lesson.

That's how I was raised, and how nonelite kids are raised today. In contrast, Lareau found that in the elite families she interviewed, kids expected adults to schedule their time and spent "a significant amount of time simply *waiting* for the next event." Lareau concludes that Tyrec, a nonelite child she featured in her study, "needs no adult assistance to pursue the great majority of his plans." Because his group of neighborhood friends "functions without adult monitoring, he learns how to construct and sustain friendships on his own," something elite kids rarely do. The informal play allowed nonelite kids "to develop skills in peer mediation, conflict management, personal responsibility, and strategizing."[132]

As a result of his greater independence, "Tyrec learned important life skills not available to [elite] Garrett. He and his friends found numerous ways of entertaining themselves, showing creativity and independence." Even sibling relationships differed. The intense focus on competition in elite families fueled intense sibling rivalry of a type rarely found in nonelite ones.[133]

Too often, in comparisons of elites to nonelites, the assumption is that nonelites should get with it and emulate their betters. That's not always true, and parenting is a case in point. Concerted cultivation and work devotion, perhaps the two central institutions of life in the professional elite, each deserves a closer look. What's the unspoken message of helicopter parenting—that if you don't knock everyone's socks off, you're a failure? What's the better message: that the key is to be a good kid, or that every child needs to be above average?

CHAPTER 8

Is the Working
Class Just Racist?

LET'S STATE RIGHT UP FRONT that racism is an issue in the white working class, and it goes back a long way.

An ugly racial dynamic arose after the Civil War when Southern elites pitted the white working class against newly freed black people by communicating that, although poor whites might be "white trash," at least they weren't black.[134] By offering poor whites the "wages of whiteness"[135]—the social dignity of membership in the dominant race—planters made them more willing to accept wages and farm tenancy contracts that left them dirt poor. This dynamic has a very long history, reaching right up to the present day. Reuel Schiller's 2015 book, *Forging Rivals,* showed that, since the New Deal, the Democratic Party's ambivalence about pursuing cross-racial coalitions generated laws that drove African-Americans and whites apart.[136] "Trump was masterful at this," mused historian Suzanne Lebsock in an email to me, "stooping to race baiting to alienate working-class whites from the black and Latino workers with whom they had the most in common."

The wages-of-whiteness strategy protected the elite from a cross-race coalition of the disenfranchised. That's the coalition America needs now: the interracial coalition for economic justice Martin Luther King, Jr., proposed a half century ago.[137] It was a difficult and controversial proposal for King then, and it hasn't gotten a lot easier. But we need to try. The first step is to ensure that we are not doing unconsciously what the post-Civil War planters did intentionally: pit working-class whites against people of color.

Elite whites do this when they comfort themselves about racism by displacing the blame for racism onto other-class whites. Julie Bettie, in her insightful study of working-class girls, observed, "[O]ne marker of having progressive politics is displaying oneself as antiracist, and this can, at times, unfortunately manifest as a demeaning of and distancing from white working-class people, who are constructed as stupid and racist."[138] Many conservatives as well as progressives do this. Commented Jacqueline Ferrara* on my *HBR* article, "Great article, but it will fall on deaf ears. The only acceptable narrative is that those who voted Republican [in 2016] did so because they are racists, sexists, stupid, or all three."

There's an element here of privileged whites distancing themselves from racism by displacing the blame for racism onto less-privileged whites. If you think you're not racist at all, drop this book and head immediately to *https://implicit.harvard.edu/implicit* to take an implicit association test.

"Everyone's a little bit racist," joked the musical *Avenue Q*, and if you're only a little, I'm impressed. About half of whites automatically prefer white people over black people.[139] Implicit association test results show that MDs, college grads, and MBAs did not score lower for implicit racial bias than did high school grads.[140]

Among liberals it's a mark of sophistication to acknowledge that everyone's a little bit racist, yet professional-class racism slides conveniently out of sight in discussions about working-class whites. Another facet of the problem is that whites from different classes are racist in quite different ways. Among the professional elite, where the coin of the realm is merit, people of color are constructed as lacking in merit. Among the white working class, where the coin of the realm is morality, people of color are constructed as lacking in that quality.

The strong antiracism norm among the PME should not be mistaken for a lack of racism. My favorite study of racism in the white-collar context is the "Greg"/"Jamal" study. The study sent out identical resumes, some with white-sounding names, some with African-American-sounding names. The study found that Jamal had to have *8 additional years* of experience to get the same number of job callbacks as Greg; the higher the quality of the resume, the stronger the racial bias became.[141]

I am part of a team (with psychology professor Richard Lee and sociologist Su Li) that developed a 10-minute Workplace Experiences Survey designed to measure workplace climate. When used in a national study of engineers, the survey found that engineers of color were more likely than white male engineers to report prove-it-again bias: engineers of color had to prove themselves over and over; other people got credit for ideas they originally offered; their ideas were less likely to be respected.[142] These self-reports confirmed that the racial bias documented by 40 years of lab studies shows up in today's professional workplaces.[143]

Working-class racism is different. First of all, it's more explicit: studies consistently show more explicit racist statements among whites without college degrees than among whites with them.[144] According to an influential study of working-class whites in Canarsie, New York, in the 1980s, these whites viewed African-Americans as lacking family values and a healthy work ethic—the same weapons settled living whites use to place themselves above both professional elites and hard-living whites. "It's really a class problem," said an educated housewife from working-class Canarsie. "I don't care about the color of a person if they're nice people. The black parents in the school programs I work with are beautiful and refined people. They're like us." What drove these Canarsie residents crazy were "ghetto" black people: "Flashy cars, booze, and broads is all they care about. They don't even want to get ahead for their families!" "Beneath the surface of apparently racial judgments was the ineluctable reality of class cultures in conflict," concluded sociologist Jonathan Rieder.[145] I see what he was saying, but it's not just a class problem: associating hard living with African-Americans—that's a brand of racism.

Whites who were antiracist, Lamont found, grounded their understandings of black people in the view that there are "good and bad people in all races,"[146] believing that hard workers of all races are equals. Said an oil company foreman:

> *No matter who you are at Exxon, you're making pretty good money, so it's not like you've got a disadvantaged person. Their kids are going to good schools. They're eating, they're taking vacations because of Exxon. You don't see the division or whatever, so Exxon kind of eliminated that because of the salary structure. . . . With black people, you talk sports, you talk school, you're all in the same boat. . . . You know, you talk to the guy, and you went on vacation, and he went on vacation.*[147]

Note the consistent logic: if you live a settled life, you're a good person.

To summarize, settled working-class whites, whose claims to privilege rest on morality and hard work, stereotype black people by conflating hard living and race. Professional-class whites, whose claims to privilege rest on merit, stereotype black people as less competent than whites. There is no excuse for either kind of racism. Here's the point: privileged whites should stop justifying their refusal to acknowledge their class privilege over less-privileged whites on the grounds that those "others" are racist.

I'm not denying that some people who voted for Trump are white supremacists. After all, one of the few newspapers to endorse him was the newspaper of the KKK. Trump's campaign rhetoric included beyond-the-pale racist statements about Mexicans, proposals to violate the Constitution by discriminating against Muslim immigrants based on religion, and a promise to build a wall between the United States and Mexico.[148]

Trump's racism also helped him with some supporters who experienced his comments as a delicious poke-in-the-eye of elites. To these supporters, Trump broke with political correctness taboos in a daring way. That's a dynamic our country can change—and has to change. The goal of mainstream politicians of both parties should be to drive a wedge between the viciousness of white supremacy and people who are basically decent but tired of what they see as "political correctness" that ignores the very considerable challenges faced by working-class whites while directing them to feel sorry for a whole range of other groups.

The first step is to avoid writing off all Trump voters. "I know these Trump voters," wrote Ben Richards, who works for the YMCA in Ann Arbor, Michigan. "Most of them are not racists or bigots or sexists or xenophobic. They simply wanted someone to fight for them, or at least appear to. These Trump voters were disgusted by his outlandish behavior and his derogatory comments." Indeed, 20% of Trump voters had an unfavorable opinion of him, and 17% of Trump voters approved of the job Obama was doing at the end of his term.[149]

These issues are complicated. One class migrant wrote to me:

> *Your article brought me to tears. . . . I was raised in a blue-collar, religious, racist, nationalistic home. I am now a flaming liberal with a master's and a high-paying cor-*

*porate job. . . . Your article deeply articulated the view of
my family in a way they never could. I don't believe they
are hateful, or racist, or stupid. They're mostly afraid.
Afraid of the brown skin people. Afraid of the day they
can't live in their own home any more. Afraid of global
economics. Afraid of those who dare claim their God is not
real. Afraid of sexually empowered women. Afraid of the
scientific utterances they can't understand related to climate
change, so they just reject it outright. Fear manifests in
many ways, but it's the same root. . . . I've also concluded
that we liberals own 99% of the responsibility for Trump's
election. It's easy to dismiss him as a con man and enu-
merate Hillary's huge list of qualifications. But she could
never connect with my WWC [white working-class] family, and Trump can. I don't blame him or his voters one
bit—he's just a con man who saw an opening, and they're
just supporting someone who gives them a voice—we're
the ones who failed. And we need to own that.*

His feelings are complex and are shared by many of the
flood of class migrants who have written to me. He acknowledges racism but doesn't believe his family members
are bad people.

His message is an important one: what his family needs
is not a lecture about racism but a conversation about fear.
"Telling people they're racist, sexist, and xenophobic is going
to get you exactly nowhere," said Alana Conner of Stanford.
"It's such a threatening message. One of the things we know
from social psychology is when people feel threatened, they

can't change, they can't listen."[150] What causes people to change their minds are conversations designed to make a connection with them, through honesty and empathy. That worked when activists canvassed to assess—and create—support for transgender rights.[151] Two-thirds of the recent sea change in acceptance of marriage equality stemmed from a gradual process of people changing their thinking.[152]

Fear of "brown people" and anti-immigrant feelings may stem from the fact that mass immigration returned to the United States in the 1970s for the first time since 1910[153]—which has coincided with the white working class's fall from blue-collar grace. It's easy to confuse correlation with causation, and there's some of that going on, associating the good old days with the old white days.

Another factor is that there has been more immigration to rural areas.[154] Jennifer Sherman found that those who remained in the rural area she studied after the local mill closed down stressed the importance of place, which "conveniently conceals their inabilities to easily adapt to unfamiliar circumstances." Fear of what lay outside the isolated valley where her subjects lived was a strong motivating factor in their decision to stay.[155] These were not people well equipped to cope with a massive influx of immigrants.

One way to help ease tensions is to create a national discourse that acknowledges and respects traditionalism and hard work, values shared by both immigrants and working-class whites. In the 1990s, Lamont found approval of immigrants for exactly these reasons.[156] A difficult challenge is that working-class whites, themselves disciplined by rules, tend to disapprove of those who don't follow them. True immigration reform would make this problem abate or disappear, but that hardly seems on the horizon.

The road will be a bumpy one, and there's a lot we can't control. One thing we can control is the elite's class condescension, which has driven working-class whites into the arms of the far right. Arlie Hochschild reflected back on Louisiana whites' sense of loss, and whom they blame. "I've had enough of *poor me*," said a mayor who started out as an instrumentation foreman at Phillips 66. "I met this one black guy who complained that he couldn't get a job. Come to find out he'd been to *private* school. I went to a local public school like everyone else I know. No one should be getting a job to fill some mandated racial quota."[157]

Note the class resentment. Because I study social inequality, I know that even Malia and Sasha Obama will be disadvantaged by race, advantaged as they are by class. But Hochschild aptly maps the sense of losing ground, the contour map of resentment. "After the 2008 crash ... some got rich, others got poor. And you didn't want the government playing favorites *on top of that*."[158] In the past roughly 20 years, the proportion of whites who felt their standard of living is worse than their parents' increased from 13% to 21%.[159] During that period, liberal "feeling rules"—norms about how one should feel—mandated sympathy for the poor, for people of color, for women, for refugees, for LGBTQ individuals.[160] Caring about working-class whites is optional—a private frolic some indulge but most don't share.

Hochschild, with her unerring sense of metaphor, sums it up. The Tea Party members she befriended in Louisiana felt like people patiently waiting in line, living settled lives that required hard work and self-discipline, only to "see people *cutting in line ahead of you!* You're following the rules. They aren't.... Some are black. Through affirmative action plans, ... jobs, welfare payments, and free lunches, ... they hold a certain secret place in people's minds.... Women, immigrants, refugees, public sector workers—where will it end?" "*I live your analogy,*" commented one of her Tea Party friends. Hochschild points out that "virtually all those I talked with felt on shaky economic ground.... They also felt culturally marginalized."[161] Their traditionalist views were held up to ridicule by the national media; they felt belittled and besieged. Referring to people like this as "deplorables," as Hillary Clinton did during the campaign,[162] is not a great way to win them back.

Many things we can't change, but here's one we can: we can communicate that we believe that the injustices experienced by working-class whites are ones elites have a moral obligation to address. It's only human to place much of the world's vast reservoir of injustice outside of one's personal ambit of responsibility. We do not immediately drop what we are doing, sell all our worldly goods, and fly to Calcutta to distribute the proceeds in the streets. Why? We see the injustice, but don't see it as our responsibility to redress. Historian Thomas Haskell's elegant study documents how slavery went from being seen as an unfortunate-but-unavoidable reality to being seen as a pressingly unethical outrage. Quite abruptly in the eighteenth century, slaves were included in Europeans' ambit of responsibility.[163]

Once white workers were placed outside liberals' ambit of responsibility, they wrote off "those below" as lacking in morals, grit, and taste. "My fellow liberals should have listened to me and other liberals from white working-class backgrounds. They should have listened to those of us they call hillbillies, rednecks, hicks, and toothless idiots. They should have understood that we don't live in a 'fly-over' state; we live in our home," commented Erin Brown.* ("Fly-over" is another casual class insult that passes for wit.)

"We try to be right-living, clean-living people," a former pipefitter told Hochschild, who also noted her friends were proud they had the "moral strength to endure"[164] and talked of "being *churched*" with as much pride as her crowd might talk about being "highly educated." They were proud of their Christian morality and deeply wounded when it was depicted as homophobic ignorance. Said one Tea Party member, "the American Dream is more than having money. It's feeling proud to be an American, and to say 'under God' when you salute the flag, and feel *good* about that. And it's about living in a society that believes in clean, normal family life."[165]

Hochschild recognizes that her Tea Party friends felt a loss not only of blue-collar jobs; they also felt a loss of blue-collar honor. "For along with blue-collar jobs, a blue-collar way of life was going out of fashion, and with it, the honor attached to a rooted self and pride in endurance." The communities they are so proud of are commonly depicted as insular and closed-minded.[166] A gospel singer told Hoch-schild how much she loved Rush Limbaugh. Hochschild was mystified until she realized that her attraction to Limbaugh stemmed from her sense that Limbaugh was defending her against insults she felt liberals were lobbing at her—that "Bible-believing Southerners are ignorant, backward, red-necks, losers. They think we're racist, sexist, homophobic, and maybe fat." Rush Limbaugh protected their pride.[167]

If you don't want to drive working-class whites to be attracted to the likes of Limbaugh, stop insulting them. More than that: seek to understand and respect the logic of their lives. Acknowledge that their folkways work as well for working-class lives as professional-class folkways work for elite ones.

Doesn't white working-class people's sense of entitlement to decent jobs reflect white privilege? Sure it does: even during the glory days, when blue-collar whites' wages were spiraling up, and the FHA was helping them buy homes, those jobs and houses were not equally available to African-Americans.[168] But for the left to dismiss white working-class demands on grounds of white privilege ... what's the mes-sage? That white working-class people aren't entitled to the American dream? Isn't the right message that *all* Americans are, regardless of race?

Another crucial step is to apply to the white working class the kind of analysis applied to other groups who face struc-tural disadvantage. We bend over backward to understand why many poor women have children very early, attentive to the structural factors that make that a logical choice and the cultural factors that make it an attractive one.[169] But when it comes to working-class whites, social structure evaporates. I have never heard anyone fault inner-city black people, and say they deserve to remain in poverty, because of their refusal to move where the jobs are. But working-class whites? Their refusal reflects "stubborn immobility."

Would working-class whites be so furious about "political correctness" if *they* were among those whose challenges were recognized? Not likely. We won't know how much racism falls away until we stop insulting working-class whites and try including them within our ambit of responsibility.

Does that mean abandoning people of color? Of course not. We must not assume a zero-sum game: that if we care about gender, we don't care about race; and if we care about race, we don't care about class. Claiming we can focus on only one issue at a time also ignores people who belong to more than one group, such as black women or working-class LGBTQ people.

There's no empirical evidence to suggest that addressing one vector of social inequality will necessarily hurt those affected by a different vector. The Workplace Experiences Survey shows that not only people of color but also women and individuals with disabilities report they have to prove themselves over and over again, much more so than majority men.[170] Addressing prove-it-again bias through structural reforms will level the playing field for everyone.

In 1967, Martin Luther King, Jr., called for an interracial coalition for economic justice, and he tried to unite a broad range of religious, civil rights, and labor groups to achieve a

"Freedom Budget." Along with traditional civil rights goals, that budget included a full-employment policy with public works jobs for those idled by capitalist boom-and-bust cycles and raising the minimum wage to a living wage.[171]

King understood that what we need to address is social inequality—all of it. Fifty years later, we still do.

CHAPTER 9

Is the Working Class Just Sexist?

IN THE 2016 U.S. presidential campaign, Hillary Clinton and her surrogates hammered again and again on the idea that breaking the "highest, hardest glass ceiling"[172] would be an historic achievement. Her planned victory celebration was even going to be held in a building with a massive glass ceiling and would feature confetti that looked like shattered glass, reinforcing that central campaign metaphor.

It was a class-clueless metaphor.

Shattering the glass ceiling means giving privileged women access to the high-level jobs now held almost exclusively by privileged men. And for many professional women, it's a meaningful dream—which is why so many of those women felt completely gutted by Clinton's loss. In her they saw a woman who, like themselves, had been forced to walk the likability/competence tightrope, who had often put her husband's career ahead of her own needs, and who, over and over again, had been held to a vastly higher standard than less qualified men. Watching her shatter that ceiling was a dream that mattered deeply to them. Indeed, a key message of the election, drowned out by all the attention to class (including by me) after the 2016 election, is that the glass ceiling is more shatter-resistant than most of us thought.

But can you explain why a white working-class audience—male or female—should care about it? They don't. It's not that the working class is more sexist. It's that gender, and gender equality, mean something different in the working-class context. Working-class women would never get near the C-suite even if they were men.

Many working-class women have the same kinds of pink-collar jobs their mothers did, but their husbands don't have the blue-collar jobs their fathers did. As a result, their families are in precarious shape economically. It is in these women's self-interest, and their families' self-interest, to get those blue-collar jobs back. The Tea Party women Hochschild met in Louisiana (virtually all of them employed or retired from jobs) based their politics on "their role as wives and mothers—and they wanted to be wives to high-earning men and to enjoy the luxury, as one woman put it, of being a homemaker."[173] Their focus was not on gender equality. A woman from the Appalachian section of Ohio said that she was voting to save her boyfriend's job.[174] "If I turned down every candidate who objectified women," a nurse observed tartly, "I'd vote for no one." "I have so many friends whose health care costs have doubled and are having to get extra jobs just to pay their insurance," observed a Chattanooga student studying to be a mortgage broker.[175] Trump won among white working-class women by 28 percentage points; if Clinton had won even 50% of their votes, she would have won the election.[176]

What working-class women see is that blue-collar jobs with good pay are heavily gendered as male; men ensure they remain so through severe sexual harassment of women who try to enter.[177] It can be porn on the walls, or a disgusting photoshopped picture in your locker. Co-workers may refuse to train you, or loosen a screw so that using a tool can maim you.[178] Not surprising, then, that most working-class white women don't aspire to "men's work." Instead, they invest more of their identity in family in a very gendered way. Arlie Hochschild summarized their feelings: "'I may not be the boss here, but I have another life where I am' ... 'I may be subordinate here, but I express myself fully at home.'"[179]

The poor quality of child care adds to the allure of stay-at-home motherhood. "For most working-class families ... child care often is patched together in ways that leave parents anxious and children in jeopardy," noted a 1994 study that described a family in which the oldest—age nine—was home alone after school. This mother said wistfully she wanted to quit but couldn't, because they needed the money.[180]

The problem has only gotten worse since 1994. Remember tag teaming from Chapter 3, where mom works one shift and dad works a different one? Here's a typical scenario, from a family with children ages 9, 2½, and 18 months, where dad is a day laborer, the mom a janitor. "By the time Manuel comes home from work, I have left for work," said Flor. "When I get home around 11:30 p.m., Manuel is asleep. The next morning at 5:00 a.m. when Manuel leaves for work, I am asleep. It doesn't give us much time together." For many working-class families, having mothers in the workforce represents not gender equality but stress and disruption. Tag-team parents divorce at three to six times the national rate.[181]

For working-class whites, and Latinos like Manuel and Flor, the breadwinner-homemaker family looks pretty good, not just for practical reasons but also for symbolic ones.

The notion that women belong at home while men went out to work emerged in the nineteenth century;[182] from the beginning, it was a key way that elites distinguished themselves from the working class. A man's ability to support his family signaled his status. Having a stay-at-home wife became something the working class aspired to. In the second half of the twentieth century, the U.S. working class attained the breadwinner-housewife ideal for two brief generations. By the twenty-first century, a new generation of workers had lost the ability to sustain the ideal they had seen their parents and grandparents achieve.[183] Small wonder many felt bereft.

Among whites, the breadwinner role unites men, but stay-at-home motherhood divides women. For working-class white women, becoming a homemaker signals a rise in status, not only for herself but for her entire family. But for PME women, becoming a stay-at-home mother entails a fall in status, from investment banker to "just a homemaker." The diminished value of caregiving in the elite is best dramatized by stay-at-home moms' painful loss of status. In a milieu where social honor stems chiefly from work devotion, telling people you are "just a housewife" can lead them literally to turn tail and flee at cocktail parties. Perhaps the best example is when a former *New York Times* reporter, after she quit to care for her baby, was asked, "Didn't you used to be Ann Crittenden?"[184]

Note that on this issue, African-American families have always been quite different. Many fewer were granted entry into the separate spheres ideal, and it held less allure. Black men have for so long been barred by racism from good jobs that many black people—both women and men—associate motherhood with both caregiving and earning.[185]

What all this means for politics is that gender does not necessarily bind women together across social class—although it can. Women share some experiences across class lines, chief among them sexual harassment. But professional-class women cannot *assume* a sisterhood with working-class women. If elite women want to create that sisterhood, they will have to create a coalition around shared interests. If the Clinton campaign had spent more time talking about Trump's sexual assaults and less time talking about the glass ceiling, they would have been far better off.

Other dynamics also weakened the appeal of Clinton's gender equality theme among white working-class women. As mentioned previously, Hochschild was initially mystified by a Louisiana woman who loved Rush Limbaugh, specifically *because* of his "criticism of 'femi-nazis,' you know, feminists, women who want to be equal with men."[186]

Hochschild gradually realized that this woman saw Limbaugh as protecting her red-state honor against blue-state belittlement. It's the same effect we saw with respect to race: Progressives have inadvertently made sexism into a way of expressing class anger. The dismissive charge of "political correctness" is a weapon forged against progressives on the anvil of their own snobbery.

What about working-class men? How much of their rapport with Trump can be dismissed as sexism? Trump was seen as standing up for real men in an economy that has deprived many working-class men of breadwinner status. Men can be winners in two different ways: they can be "good men," or "real men." A good man reflects a gender-neutral concept of decency: being considerate, moral, and honest, for example. What's a real man? "Take charge; be authoritative." "Take risks." "It means suppressing any kind of weakness."[187] Trump to a T.

The Clinton campaign could have countered this definition but didn't use weapons handed to them on a silver platter. Trump's sharp business practices have hurt blue-collar men when he stiffed the blue-collar guys who worked on his buildings. How about the Philadelphia cabinet builder Edward Friel, Jr., whose business eventually had to close after Trump refused to pay a large bill for work building the bases for slot machines at Trump Plaza?[188] Friel or someone like him should have been at Clinton rallies across the country.

Instead of mobilizing themes that could have appealed to working-class men and women, the Clinton campaign stuck to two main talking points: that Clinton had the resume to be president and Trump was unfit to lead. Straight out of the feminist playbook I, myself, helped write. In a 2014 book I wrote with Rachel Dempsey, *What Works for Women at Work*, we pointed out that women need to provide far more evidence of competence than do white men in order to be seen as equally competent.[189] So Hillary proved her competence over and over and tried to show Trump's lack of credentials.

But prove-it-again bias is only one form of gender bias—and not the most common.[190] Tightrope bias stems from prescriptive stereotypes that mandate that women[191] should be team players, helpful, modest, sympathetic, and nice. This kind of behavior, expected of women, gets you liked—but not respected.[192] Being both respected and liked is extremely difficult to pull off if you're doing a masculine thing like running for president. The most successful strategy is to try to do a masculine thing in a feminine way. Clinton did this immaculately well in the first debate, with all the smiles and that famous shimmy. But I suspect she got tired of playing Ms. Nicey Smiley. Since she was ahead in the polls, she returned to what felt more comfortable, stressing her credentials and attacking Trump. Likeability was a big problem for Clinton.

If Clinton had a likeability problem, Trump had an unlikeability epidemic—but it didn't matter.[193] Likeability is optional for men, but it's mandated for women: if a woman isn't nice, she's a bad person. ("Lock her up!") A man can be unlikeable and still be seen as a man to be reckoned with. Trump was a real man. Clinton? A nasty woman.

No doubt working-class men felt threatened by the change that Clinton symbolized and promised more of. As working-class people, they value stability and tradition—including gender traditions—rather than gender flux. Moreover, men in general, and working-class men in particular, tend to ramp up displays of manliness when their masculinity is threatened.[194] This effect will emerge to the extent that working-class men feel embattled as breadwinners and belittled as men. Many feel both.

Does Trump's victory signal that working-class men are sexist? It's not as simple as that. When it comes to gender equality, elite men tend to talk the talk but don't walk the walk; working-class men walk the walk but do not talk the talk. For example, the average working-class man is less likely to espouse egalitarian than his professional-class counterpart; but he spends more time caring for his children than does his elite counterpart.[195]

In one study, blue-collar emergency medical technicians were far more involved in family life than were white-collar physicians. They shared children's daily care in ways the doctors did not: they picked up kids from school, fed them dinner, stayed home when they were sick. Some turned down overtime completely: "Family comes first for me," said one, repeating the common working-class refrain. Many regularly consulted with their wives before accepting overtime, and turned down shifts when their wives objected, in sharp contrast to the physicians. Emergency medical technicians regularly swapped shifts to accommodate their family demands, and many "seemed *happy* with their schedules *because* they allowed the EMTs to participate in childcare."[196]

Jennifer Sherman also found shifting attitudes toward gender roles among the working class in the rural California community she studied. Being a good man had been redefined as jobs left the community. Back when the mill was going strong, being a good man meant providing for your family; if you went out and drank with the guys and slapped the wife around a bit—not a problem. No longer. As jobs became scarcer, and more and more men were permanently unemployed, families redefined being a good man as being a good father, which was defined in terms of contributing to children's care, and keeping off drugs and alcohol. Domestic violence was no longer tolerated.[197]

At the other end of the class spectrum, a survey of Harvard Business School MBAs found that elite men still have fairly traditional views of whose career should take precedence. Robin Ely, Pamela Stone, and Colleen Ammerman summarized their research thus:

> *More than half the men in Generation X and the Baby Boom said that when they left HBS, they expected that their careers would take priority over their spouses' or partners'.... Notably, this expectation was less prevalent among men of color than among white men. Forty-eight percent of the former—compared with 39% of white men—anticipated that their spouses' careers would be of equal importance. Meanwhile, the vast majority of women across racial groups and generations anticipated that their careers would rank equally with those of their partners.[198]*

Elite men can talk the talk of gender equality because they know in their bones that their careers will deliver them dignity (male varietal). Economic power, both inside the family and in the society at large, is their trump card.

I am not saying there is no sexism in the working class. I'm just saying that sexism is a pervasive problem that crosses class lines. Deflecting blame for sexism onto the working class may be comforting. Just don't mistake comfort food for insight.

10

Don't They Understand that Manufacturing Jobs Aren't Coming Back?

LET'S GET REAL. Many of those blue-collar jobs lost over the past half century, and at an increasing rate during the Great Recession, are gone forever. Globalization means that capital flows quickly to countries with the lowest wages, and it flows so quickly that companies that left the United States for China are now leaving China, where wages have risen, for lower-cost countries like Vietnam. And importantly, although the problem of companies "sending jobs overseas" has become a populist rallying cry, advances in automation and productivity are actually responsible for much of the decline in manufacturing work.[199] Making steel just doesn't require as many people as it used to.

Is the only alternative a universal basic income? This proposal,[200] currently chic among the tech set, will only further fuel the anger of working-class whites. What they want is not a social safety net but a job.

Even in a globalizing, automating world, that's not nuts—and shouldn't be impossible. But it will require new thinking by both conservatives and liberals. Liberals will have to move beyond their singular focus on the college degree as the avenue to economic achievement. Conservatives will have to recognize that providing jobs that yield a modest middle-class life for non-college grads will necessitate the kind of industrial policy that exists in Germany but has long been lacking in the United States.

An important priority is addressing the severe shortage of Americans trained for middle-skill jobs. "Friends who work in the U.S. (in water infrastructure) always complain to me about the poor skills of the average American workers they get. Trump would best start there," commented John Verhoeven.* Middle-skill jobs typically pay $40,000 and up and require some post-secondary education but not a college degree. One effect of the excessive focus on college degrees is that the United States lacks people with mid-level skills. One study found "a lack of adequate middle-skills talent directly or significantly affected the productivity of 47% of manufacturing companies, 35% of health care and social assistance companies, and 21% of retail companies." A 2011 survey found 30% of all companies and 43% of manufacturing ones had positions that had been open for 6 months that they could not fill. A more recent survey confirmed large gaps, especially in health care, technical sales, sales management, and in jobs that require computer and mathematical skills.[201]

The new manufacturing economy, concluded the MIT Task Force on Production in the Innovation Economy, requires "training for jobs that demand new combinations of book learning, hands-on experience, proficiency with digital technology, and ability to manage relationships face to face and with distant collaborators."[202] This is not what our educational system typically delivers.

Vocational training was an integral part of the high school curriculum until the 1950s, and all students were routinely taught (on a gender-segregated basis) job-ready skills along with other subjects. In the 1950s, tracking emerged that, in theory, separated students according to ability; in fact, less affluent students and students of color were tracked into vocational programs that were seen as strictly second class.[203] The response was to abolish vocational programs, on the theory that every child deserved the best—to go to college.

This strategy was self-delusion. Not everyone wants to go to college, and even those who'd like to go can't always garner the resources to accomplish this goal. Two-thirds of Americans don't graduate from college, as we've seen. The decline of vocational education has meant that American employers can't depend on a stream of employees with the specific skills they need. Employers have responded by "up credentialing" requiring college degrees for jobs that do not require college-delivered skills—as a way to weed out those who lacked the smarts or self-discipline to complete a college degree. This up-credentialing has two bad effects. Using college as a proxy for diligence and smarts, of course, disadvantages working-class kids who are smart and diligent but not college grads. It also means that a significant proportion of college grads do jobs that don't really require college. As a result, a quarter of college grads and advanced degree holders will work for a lower median wage than associate degree holders.[204]

Too often today, college education serves as a finishing school for elite kids, who go there at 18 and study full time until age 22, building the credentials and entrepreneurial networks that will see them through life. This works for elite kids but not for many working-class kids. For those who do attend college, significant changes are needed. Arizona State University President Michael Crow has led the way in making the resources of a major research university more user-friendly for children of the working class. ASU now provides online courses and scheduling options that fit better with working-class lives. Online students typically take only two or three classes per semester, and most courses cover a semester's worth of material in just seven and a half weeks. ASU provides a mentor to help students plan and navigate their college careers, which levels the playing field by providing nonelite students with the kind of advice and savvy that elite kids get from their parents.[205]

At a deeper level, what's needed is a very different kind of education-to-employment system. Its key elements were outlined in 2015 by a task force convened by the Markle Foundation. Companies need to better define what skills they need, and develop private-public alliances to develop a local talent supply chain. High schools, community colleges, and universities should work with local businesses and with unions to develop educational and training programs that lead to industry-recognized certifications that provide employers the assurance that a worker has specific skills needed for specific jobs. Beyond high school, the programming should be relatively short; flexible and part-time programming works best for adults who are working and caring for families at the same time as they are continuing their educations.[206] "And how do you propose they go back to school and pay for it if they don't have a job? That is the Catch-22," remarked Bill Parks.* The educational system that works well for the professional elites does not reflect the realities of working-class lives. What's needed are targeted, fit-for-purpose credential programs. Participants trained for a job that then disappears could return to train for a job that's just being created.

Creating a smooth education-to-employment pipeline is not a new idea. Over 70 years ago, the International Brotherhood of Electrical Workers and the National Electrical Contractors Association worked in partnership to create a training program, delivered through local affiliates, combining apprenticeships, remote online education, and personal coaching. The program has enabled hundreds of thousands of workers to earn credentials as wiremen or installers.[207] This is a key role unions could play if, alas, they were not so embattled they need to spend disproportionate resources on just trying to survive.

Another example is the Automotive Technical Education Collaborative (AMTEC), a partnership between Toyota and a local community college that has grown into a network of 30 community colleges and 34 auto-related plants in 12 states. If someone has the AMTEC credential, "it's a validation," said a manager at a local Nissan plant; employers know what to expect. The credential does not require a college degree.[208]

The Golden Triangle Link provides a third model. It's a private economic development coalition in Mississippi led by an Arkansas developer and Brenda Lathan, a black woman he promoted from the reception desk to be his director for business research and development. The Link connects local, state, and country governments, utilities, engineering companies, and local educational institutions (Mississippi State and East Mississippi Community College). In conjunction with the Center for Manufacturing Technology Excellence, which trains local people for skilled jobs managing computerized robot-heavy modern factory jobs, the Link has brought more than $4.6 billion in investment and 5,600 jobs to impoverished northeastern Mississippi.[209]

These are just illustrative examples of the ways in which educational opportunities can be restructured to provide the working class with meaningful skills. Doubtless there are others. My main point is that elites need to stop implying or stating that the working class should accept its diminished status, and start talking instead of steps toward jobs that provide a modest middle-class life.

The truism that manufacturing has fled the United States for good can be exaggerated. There are strategic, bottom-line reasons to keep manufacturing local. Take Boeing. In the early 2000s, Boeing shifted massively to outsourcing production of its new 787 Dreamliner aircraft, replacing its traditional hub-and-spoke supply chain around Seattle with about 50 production hubs around the world responsible for wings, engine, and so forth.[210] Only final assembly remained in Seattle.

Global outsourcing resulted in quality breakdowns and cost overruns. In a product where millimeters matter, the components produced in other countries were not quite right, and quality control issues plagued the plane for years. The launch was delayed, and cost overruns were enormous. A strike added to Boeing's woes. Its stock price sank so low that it took 6 years for it to recover.

In a 2011 speech, the CEO reflected, "We spent a lot more money in trying to recover than we ever would have spent if we'd tried to keep the key technologies closer to home." In 2013, Boeing reversed course. It announced it was moving wing production back to Seattle and investing in a new factory and training there. It would continue to produce some parts abroad but "we need to bring it back to a more prudent level."[211]

Commerce is getting both more global *and* more local. 3-D printing and other technologies pave the way for a new generation of niche products tailored to individual consumers and delivered with high-quality customer service. Liam Casey is incubating hardware start-ups that provide high-value products for which low-cost labor is not a key factor. "It's more important that producer and customer are close to each other," he remarked.[212] This adaptation of the German model—make the best products, not the cheapest—holds the potential for new industry in the heartland. So does the fact that major producers like IKEA and Emerson are moving to regional manufacturing to solve transportation problems.[213]

These programs provide the model for the future of working-class jobs that yield a solid middle-class standard of living. But instead of nurturing a new industrial policy, too often what the white working class hears is the prescription that working-class men should take the kinds of low-wage jobs working-class women hold. That's not the right message, as I explain in the next chapter.

11

Why Don't Working-Class Men Just Take "Pink-Collar" Jobs?

MANLY DIGNITY is highly important to working-class men, and they're not feeling it. Breadwinner status is a big part of this: Many men (of all classes) still measure masculinity by the size of a paycheck.[214] Since 1970, professional-elite wages have increased dramatically, while the wages of high-school-educated men fell 47%.[215] The percentage of men so discouraged they are not looking for work has tripled since the 1960s.[216]

Look, I wish manliness worked differently. But most men, like most women, seek to fulfill the ideals they've grown up with. For many blue-collar men, all they're asking for is basic human dignity (male varietal). When it comes to masculine dignity, men of all classes are united in their opinion: they're all for it. But members of the PME have been remarkably tone deaf in their scorn for the dignity aspirations of working-class men.

Instead, while elite men still enjoy a virtual stranglehold on highly paid high-status jobs themselves, some in the PME have recommended that blue-collar men take pink-collar jobs like genetic counselors, occupational assistants, or nurse practitioners. Highbrow discourse on Bloomberg.com and elsewhere identifies the key problem for working-class men as their outdated notions of masculinity.[217]

"They are little man-boys who need 'manly' jobs and go crying to their mamas when they have to answer to a 'woman in a pants suit' or need to perform a task that doesn't involve lifting 100 pounds or cutting through steel plates," one man opined in an email. Said another, "Swallow your pride/dignity and go back to school, get a 21st century job. Economies change. Real men and women with integrity don't expect to be handed a job or scapegoat others who get something they don't," commented Jerry Day.*

I'm all for men of all classes developing new and healthier masculinities, but to have the elite telling working-class men to abandon the breadwinner masculinity privileged men still enjoy ... that's not going to persuade working-class men of anything except that they really, really, really hate feminism. When elite men start flooding into traditionally feminine jobs, elites will have the standing to tell working-class men to swallow their masculine pride and do so, too.

And yet we do all need to recognize that twenty-first-century jobs will differ from twentieth-century ones. What's a path forward? Let's begin with a question: What's a job that requires intensive scientific training and heavy lifting?

Nursing. I'll bet that's not what came to mind. When we think of nursing, we think of the womanly art of caring, of holding the hand of the sick. Because it's feminized, nursing is persistently undervalued and underpaid. Indeed, nursing shortages have continued because of hospitals' refusal to do what's typically done when there's a shortage—pay more. That's the kind of thing that happens in a pink-collar ghetto. The solution is not to consign working-class men to the underpaid, dead-end jobs traditionally provided to women. The solution is to create up-skilled jobs for both men and women.

Here's an example, again from the Markle report. The Tablet Pilot of the New York Paraprofessional Healthcare Institute equips home health care aides with tablets that enable them to assess client health risks and communicate with doctors and other members of a patient's health care team. Armed with networked tablets, the home care workers answer 15 screening questions to monitor for documented health care risks. The pilot materially improved the quality of health care, because it addressed a key problem: often several days would pass before home aides' observations were effectively communicated to the doctor or nurse in charge. This led to false alarms and unnecessary, and expensive, trips to the ER. The Tablet Pilot decreased unnecessary hospital visits.[218]

The Tablet Pilot points the way for working-class jobs. What's needed are networked service jobs that allow for up-skilling of workers who, because they will be adding more value, will be paid more.

The technology exists to generalize this model. Today most services are seen as inherently local, but networks make that less true. Using Microsoft's HoloLens, a reporter called an electrician who then talked him through how to install a light switch. A Los Angeles company called DAQRI has developed a "smart helmet" that can allow a soldier to see a schematic drawing of a machine he needs to fix along with a step-by-step description of how to fix it. The smart helmet and HoloLens open the way to next-gen "doctors' visits" that occur in the patient's home.[219] Or to the practice of medicine in rural areas by doctors in large cities who practice in partnership with local physician assistants acting as the doctor's eyes and ears.

Some of the occupations expected to grow are ones that blue-collar guys (and gals) would likely be happy to do: wind turbine techs, cartographers, and ambulance drivers.[220] This sort of thing has not been at the center of liberals' social reform agenda, to say the least. Putting it there would require a cultural shift. Blue-collar jobs carry social prestige elsewhere, for example, in Germany, but not in the United States. "Nobody coming out of college these days is knowledgeable or excited about … [manufacturing]," said a Flextronics manager in Fort Worth. A community college student commented, if manufacturing "was a last resort I'd probably have to go in, but that's definitely not what I want to be doing."[221]

These attitudes have consequences. For example, there's a shortage of plumbers so acute that it's threatening the building industry. Plumbers can make good money—the national median is $60,000 a year for a master plumber, but in a large city a plumber can make six figures.[222] "My plumber drives a Porsche," noted a friend. Are lame jokes about "plumber's butt" worth the economic price our country pays for looking down on this kind of work?

It's time to reverse that attitude. "I haven't heard either party talking about a 'real' jobs program or a 'real' training program. Most of the centers that are supposed to do this kind of work do very surface level training like how to write a resume, how to do an online job search, etc.," wrote Elizabeth Ringler-Jayanthan. That's a pressing social issue. Let's treat it like one.

Why Don't the People Who Benefit Most from Government Help Seem to Appreciate It?

BY 2008, my father-in-law was in bad shape. His dementia was so advanced that my mother-in-law sorely needed some respite. We found a day care program and suggested she inquire whether government subsidies were available to help cover the cost. A lifelong Democrat, she initially dismissed the suggestion out of hand. "It's not worth it. The government doesn't care about people like us, who have worked all their lives. They only care about the poor."

She asked, though, and—quickly and efficiently—Medicare covered the costs.

Since then I've been on a quiet rampage. When she received a new energy-efficient refrigerator that, to her delight, cost her only $100, I pointed out that it was compliments of the Obama stimulus program.[223] When fire fighters came to her house to check her smoke alarms and make sure the house was safe, I gently pointed out that that, too, was a government benefit. When she marveled one day that she had a full meal at the senior center for only $3, again I mentioned that the bounty she's enjoying comes from her government.

This should not be a one-woman campaign.

In Suzanne Mettler's must-read book *The Submerged State*, she points out that most Americans don't know about the subsidies and benefits they receive from their government. In 2008, a survey asked Americans whether they had "ever used a government social program, or not." Of those surveyed, 56.5% said they never had. In fact, 91.6% had.[224]

For the working class, the most valuable and least discussed social program is the system of disability payments to those deemed unable to work (formally known as Social Security Disability Insurance). Chana Joffe-Walt's reporting, which has received shockingly little attention, documented that the federal government spends more on cash payments for disability than on food stamps and Temporary Assistance to Needy Families (aka "welfare") combined.[225] Nearly 40% of men aged 21–64 were on disability in the rural California community Sherman studied.[226]

Joffe-Walt documents the steep increase in the costs of the disability program and its link to the disappearance of blue-collar jobs. She spoke with a doctor who, when deciding whether to certify disability, always asks patients what grade they finished in school, which "is not really a medical question. But Dr. Timberlake believes he needs this information in disability cases because people who have only a high school education aren't going to be able to get a sit-down job."[227] Dr. Timberlake was hesitant to deny disability to someone who was unlikely to be able to find work.

She also spoke with a man in Washington, whose "dad had a heart attack and went back to work in the mill. If there'd been a mill for [the son] to go back to work in, he says, he'd have done that too." But the mill had closed, so the son went on disability. In his 50s, he went to lots of meetings about retraining programs, but finally a staff member pulled him aside and advised: "There's nobody gonna hire you.... Just suck all the benefits you can out of the system until everything is gone, and then you're on your own." The system lacks incentives for retraining and disincentives for relocation. It has become "a de facto welfare program for people without a lot of education or job skills," Joffe-Walt concluded, that consigns them to permanent poverty. It pays $13,000 a year. "Once people go onto disability, they almost never go back to work."[228]

Yes, I get the irony: the white working class is outraged about welfare but benefiting from a different welfare program themselves. If we actually had a robust industrial policy and effective job retraining, we'd be far better off. But we also need something else: a new public understanding of government programs and who benefits from them.

One reason working-class whites associate the government only with subsidies for the poor is that many subsidies for the middle class are submerged—visible only to policy specialists (I learned this in grad school at MIT). These include the mortgage interest deduction, student loans, and tax exemptions for retirement and health benefits. In 2007, the Home Mortgage Interest Deduction cost taxpayers four times as much as Section 8 public housing subsidies,[229] but knowing that is the province of specialists.

Many Americans don't even know that Medicare is a federal program. A man stood up at a 2009 town hall held by Rep. Robert Inglis (R-SC) and told him to "Keep your government hands off my Medicare." Inglis politely explained, "Actually, sir, your health care is being provided by the government.'" Inglis told the *Huffington Post*, "But he wasn't having any of it."[230] Similarly, when Trump took office, some celebrated the repeal of "Obamacare," which they saw as a government welfare program, not realizing it was the same as the "Affordable Care Act."[231]

Whose fault is that?

Conservatives have engaged in a sustained, decades-long effort to popularize negative attitudes toward government. They have been tragically successful. Only 19% of Americans say they can trust government always or most of the time, which is among the lowest levels in the past half century. Only 20% say government programs are well run. But when asked about programs one by one, Americans see a major role for government not only in keeping the country safe from terrorism (94%) and responding to natural disasters

(88%) but also in ensuring safe food and medicine (87%), protecting the environment (75%), strengthening the economy (74%), and setting workplace standards (66%).[232]

How do those attitudes fit together? When Arlie Hochschild traveled to Louisiana to find out why Tea Party members were so hostile to government in one of the most polluted regions in the world, she found—no surprise—that hostility to government was fueled by programs for the poor. Nationwide, only 36% of Republicans say government should have a major role in addressing poverty.[233]

Publicizing to working-class Americans how they themselves benefit from government programs needs to be a major priority. Not just for liberals: my sense is that many moderate conservatives now feel that hostility to government has gone too far. We need a bipartisan campaign to educate the American public about the positive roles that government plays in their lives. There are two major themes that will appeal to the white working class (and many others): keeping them safe and ensuring economic stability.

Both white and black working-class men see protecting their families as a key part of keeping their world in moral order (see Table 1).[234] Governments help them do this. Local and state governments supply police and firefighters, who protect their homes and families. The federal government protects citizens through the military and FBI. State and federal environmental agencies protect citizens from toxins and pollution. The Food and Drug Administration ensures food safety, which is no mean feat, and protects us from unsafe drugs.[235] The Federal Trade Commission protects against identity theft and against those scammers who swindle grand-mas. All this we take for granted; it makes news only when an agency messes up.

Federal and state governments also ensure economic stability for working-class families. Thanks to Social Security,[236] Medicare,[237] and (through Obamacare) pre-scription drug benefits,[238] the elderly have the lowest pov-erty rate of any age group. (Children have the highest poverty rate.[239])

Another fruitful theme is the way the federal govern-ment has helped make the United States uniquely prosper-ous and innovative. Nearly two-thirds of Americans own their homes thanks to the FHA, Fannie Mae, and other en-tities that are run, or were founded and nurtured, by the federal government.[240] Our scientists make breakthroughs important for people throughout the world, due to support from the National Institutes of Health and National Science Foundation. The Agricultural Research Service developed strains of super-grains that have helped the poor the world over escape starvation, and the Cooperative Extension Ser-vice gives America's extraordinarily productive farmers the know-how they need to produce abundant food.

Two-thirds of Americans say government has a negative effect on the ways things are going in this country. But 56% believe the same thing about large corporations.[241] This suggests a potentially useful theme for people interested in restoring faith in government. Americans need govern-ment to protect them against overweening corporate power. Without the federal government, bankers would refuse affordable loans to working-class kids for college, and to vets who want to get an education or buy homes. Without government supervision, insurance companies refused to give health insurance to hardworking Americans with pre-existing conditions. And banks jacked up secret fees until the Consumer Financial Protection Bureau required the banks to pay them back.[242]

The appetite for a fairer playing field is out there. Arlie Hochschild found that Louisiana Tea Party members were also outraged by what scholars call "regulatory capture"— when regulators become more favorable to the industries they're supposed to be overseeing than the ordinary people they're supposed to be protecting. Said a Tea Partier, "The health unit came down on my *nephew* for not keeping his hogs away from the bad water, but they *didn't do nothing about the bad water.*" Said another, "The state always seems to come down on the *little* guy" while letting large corporations off the hook. Notes Hochschild, "It was becoming easier to understand why energy refugees were so furious at the state government."[243] (By energy refugees, she means Louisianans driven out of their homes due to pollution or other externalized costs of local energy industries.)

Yes, government regulation can be a pain. If you run a small business, which many working-class people do, regulations can pose a bewildering series of hoops you have to jump through, administered by those professionals the working class often resents. And corporations will always loudly blame government regulation for an unpopular product (energy-efficient lightbulbs) or to deflect attention from corporate failures. Americans are going to hear, and experience first-hand, ways in which government regulation is vexing. But this makes it all the more important to have a counter-narrative. Because if we have none, well, then there's no counter-narrative. People will only see the downside of regulation and not the upside.

There's another counter-narrative to the "common knowledge" that the government screws up everything. The military, a highly respected institution among working-class whites, does a good job of providing many services that government supposedly cannot provide well, notably child care.[244] (Alas, the waiting time fiascos at the VA are not helping the agency's reputation.)

It will take a sustained effort to change Americans' attitude toward government—but then it took a long time to get where we are today.[245] Millions of dollars have been spent teaching Americans to distrust their government. It's time for some spending to point out all the ways government at every level, and particularly the federal government, helps the have-a-littles, not just the have-nots. Changing working-class attitudes will require a mind shift for progressives whose instinct has been to highlight the benefits of government help for the poor. Again, that strategy only hurts the poor—and everyone else—in the long run.

A little information goes a long way. Mettler describes a 2007 study in which Americans were given information about which groups benefited from the Earned Income Tax Credit (EITC). Afterwards, 68% of respondents said that the program should be expanded.[246] (It's important to remember that the EITC helps families *who are working*. I doubt the same result would have been reached if people were asked about TANF and food stamps.)

Mettler argues against tax expenditures—subsidies delivered through the tax code—and for direct government provisioning. She also suggests redesigning government procedures that make government subsides more salient. I think it was great that the Obama administration shifted student loans away from banks to the government,[247] and that the Consumer Financial Protection Bureau has been active in advocating on students' behalf.[248] But tax expenditures and privatization are here to stay, alas, because both make it easier to assemble a legislative coalition.[249]

A while back, I floated the idea of an internet campaign modeled on the highly influential "It Gets Better" Project, in which people post short videos about their own lives designed to reassure gay youth that they have a future worth living for. I proposed to have Americans make short videos of their daily lives, thanking the government for some service or benefit that makes those lives possible—highways, the internet, sewer systems, schools, etc., and ending with the phrase, "Thank you, Uncle Sam!" No funding's come through yet, but I still think this has potential.[250]

The final thing we need to do is reinstitute civics. When I was growing up, everyone took a civics course. It gave a distinctly celebratory view of American institutions: the Constitution and separation of powers, the Bill of Rights' guarantees of freedom of speech and religion, the presumption of innocence, and trial by jury. By the time I got to college, the new social history shifted to social movements and oppressed groups. That shaped the way American school children are taught history. Celebrating our democracy went out of fashion.

When Trump railed that he was going to put Hillary in jail, that didn't sound un-American to many voters. Having a president summarily jail a defeated opponent violates separation of powers, trial by jury, and the presumption of innocence. The fact that more voters were not repulsed by Trump's statements is linked, I believe, to the demise of civics. It's time to bring back the teaching of American values. We can do so without descending into jingoism or nationalism.

I have devoted my life to gender and race issues; I'm not suggesting that we abandon the social history curriculum completely. But we need to make sure all Americans know not only the ways our system has failed but also the ways it's succeeded—if progressives want to keep the social gains we've made in the past 50 years.

Part of the reason I'm convinced that we can improve Americans' views of government is because patriotism is so important to the white working class. J. D. Vance notes that his grandmother "always had two gods: Jesus Christ and the United States of America. I was no different, and neither was anyone else we knew."[251] Patriotism is out of fashion in the PME, especially among liberals, but remains robust in working-class circles. Being American is one of the only high-status categories they belong to.[252] We all stress the high-status social categories we belong to. I remember

discussing this with a feminist friend, who smiled as she recalled showing up at an important job interview "dripping
with pearls."[253] She may have been a less plausible candidate
as a woman, but she made sure her prospective employers
knew she was connected to the kind of people who bought
pearls. Lots of them.

CHAPTER 13

Can Liberals Embrace
the White Working
Class without
Abandoning Important
Values and Allies?

"SHOULD THE PARTY continue tailoring its message to the fast-growing young and nonwhite constituencies that propelled President Obama, or make a more concerted effort to win over the white voters who have drifted away?" asked *The New York Times*.[254] In anxious emails with my friends, the most common fears are that all the talk about the white working class will come at the expense of groups who have been at the center of the progressive imagination: people of color, LGBTQ people, immigrants, women. A class migrant who made a career as a partner in a large law firm wrote that after Trump's election, her younger brother and others were "thrilled that they do not need to be PC in public anymore." When she got "very upset," her brother said, "boy, you really do live in a very different world."

My strongest message is this: business-as-usual isn't working. Is the LGBTQ community better off with Jeff Sessions as attorney general, who as a senator received a 0% rating from the Human Rights Campaign?[255] Are people of color better off with a president who was endorsed by the official newspaper of the KKK?[256] Are immigrants better off with a president who has described them as criminals and rapists? Are women better off in a world with a president that sexually assaults women and brags about it?

This is where class cluelessness has brought us.

It's inaccurate to assume that connecting with working-class whites necessarily entails abandoning progressives' traditional allies. Take people of color. In the 2016 election, communities of color split. Only 8% of African-Americans voted for Trump, but 29% of Latinos did,[257] and the Hispanic voting bloc keeps expanding.[258] Why did almost a third of Latinos vote for Trump, more than voted for Romney in 2012?

Many Latinos are "values voters," offended by the shock-the-bourgeois avant-garde element of elite culture. "For many Hispanic Americans, the cultural changes of the past 15 years have been very hard. Trump, for many, is a return to the mother's womb," said Roberto Rodríguez Tejera, who runs a Spanish-language talk show in South Florida. Some Latino citizens fear that undocumented immigrants will take their jobs; roughly a quarter of Latinos favor Trump's wall. Polls show that Latino voters care about many of the issues the white working class cares about, notably jobs and terrorism.[259] Learning how to talk respectfully with the white working class will help Democrats reach Latino voters, too.

Ending class cluelessness also would help Democrats better connect with working-class black people. Working-class black people share with professional-class liberals the view that social disadvantage is deeply structural, but in most ways they are more similar to working-class whites. When sociologist Michèle Lamont made a table comparing black and white working-class men, most values overlapped: Hardworking, Responsible, Providing, Protecting, Personal Integrity, Straightforwardness/Sincerity, and Traditional Morality (see Table 1).

The guiding principles of the progressive coalition reflect what the PME wants, not what the broad range of African-Americans want. Wrote a friend, "The truth is most blacks are pretty conservative socially—something that is seldom discussed. But I think our history is such that while we may not support abortion, LGBT and other social issues, we believe that liberals will hurt us less than other groups. Sad but true."

Ending class cluelessness will also help a small but important group of people of color: class migrants. While on a book tour in 2010, I discussed how education can drive a painful wedge between upwardly mobile class migrants and their families. The students who came up to me after my talks at universities, some in tears, were chiefly students of color. "No one's ever recognized this about me," was the general sentiment. *Of course*, if you think about it, many students of color at elite schools are undergoing the angst-filled process of choosing between the traditions of their families and those of the professional elite. Ending class cluelessness will make it easier for class migrants of all races to get their share of the American dream.

Many challenges lie ahead, including tensions between the goals and values of the white working class and the existing progressive coalition. Let's begin with an important principle: a coalition is not a mind meld. We can work together without agreeing on every single thing.

During one of George W. Bush's presidential campaigns, I went to help get out the vote for the Democratic candidate in Ohio, where substantial tensions existed between African-Americans and the LGBTQ community. Many black churches were urging voters to vote against ordinances prohibiting discrimination against gays. Democrats, of course, did not throw black voters out of their coalition because many are social conservatives. The party supported *both* gay rights *and* African-American rights. In Ohio, we did not back down from gay rights. But neither did we rub gay rights in African-Americans' faces at every turn.

A coalition is like a family in two ways. First, it involves trading. If you get your way on this, I'll get my way on that. That's the glue that keeps a coalition together. A coalition's like a family in another way, too. We need to cut one another some slack. When you show up for Thanksgiving dinner, you don't shove your political views down Aunt Josie's throat; that would signal to her that you don't value your relationship with her. And it would signal to your family that you don't value your relationship with them.

I recognize that it's hard to cut anyone slack when what you're arguing about is perceived as a human rights issue. This is true in the abortion debate (for both sides); the debates over LGBTQ rights; the debates over race and religion and gender and so many other debates in American life today. While framing these debates as human rights issues has been effective in many ways, it has also come at a cost. Human rights rhetoric was invented originally as a language to communicate that genocide and crimes against humanity are always immoral.[260] That's what gave the rhetoric its "there's no compromise possible here" tone and carried the message that human rights should always have top priority.

But this Manichean construction holds substantial risks for coalitions. Most political issues are not like ripping dissenters' fingernails out or obliterating entire populations. Often they involve a clash of sincerely held beliefs held by fundamentally decent people. Healthy politics requires being able to reach working compromises so we can all live together, despite the fact that we see diametrically opposed truths as indisputably true.

The working class—of all races—has been asked to swallow a lot of economic pain while elites have focused on noneconomic issues: this is the first generation in American history to experience lifetime downward mobility compared with people their age a decade before.[261] In 1970, 90% of 30-year-olds earned more than their parents at the same age; by 2014, only half did.[262] Neither party has taken effective steps to stop this precipitous slide. "Rural America is in a deep, deep depression that has been completely ignored by both Democrats and Republicans," commented Frank Philllips.* It's time to pay attention.

Obviously, reframing American liberal politics is a complex and long-term proposition. Here are some suggestions on specific issues.

Trade policy. It's not a good idea to embrace a trade deal that's good for the country as a whole, but bad for people working in specific industries without providing for job training for people in those industries. I'm no expert, but my friend Joel Paul is. "We live in a world in which capital can move easily across borders but workers can't, so workers always get the short end of the stick in free trade agreements," he told me. In roughly the decade after 2000, more than 42,000 U.S. factories closed, some due to recession; but most moved overseas. Around 6 million manufacturing jobs were lost. The most straightforward approach is, as part of the trade treaty, to have the U.S. government give vouchers to finance retraining in communities that lose many jobs. In 2015 house Democrats voted down a provision in Obama's trade program that provided assistance to displaced workers.[263] Typical support is for one semester in community college—"not enough so that the machinist can retrain as a plumber," Paul pointed out. We've also built into our tax code incentives for companies to move overseas. Changing the tax code and trade adjustment vouchers should both be bipartisan objectives.[264]

Abortion. Kristin Luker's 1984 study found most pro-choice advocates were college graduates who had incomes in the top 10% of working women, whereas pro-life women were less likely to be employed, earned less when they were, and were married to blue-collar workers or small business owners.[265] The abortion debate is about gender, but it's also about class conflict.

To many in the working class, abortion signals the elite's obsession with self-development and self-actualization, its idolatry of work, and the professional class's devaluation of family life. As the abortion rights movement has gradually learned, the best slogans are not "My Body, My Choice"—too self-focused to resonate outside the movement—but "Pro-Child, Pro-Choice, Pro-Family." Anyone who truly values healthy families should support the choices of adults who don't want children. Raising them is rewarding but difficult—so difficult that everyone who values families should help ensure that adults who don't want kids don't have them. This framing won't resolve the conflict, but at least it deflates the argument that abortion rights are anti-family.

Immigration. Anti-immigrant sentiment is very real; the first step is to attend to the economic woes of the working class. An important message is that immigrants typically do jobs whites don't want, from backbreaking farm work to bussing tables. Many working-class whites have a stake in immigration reform. Small business owners will be hurt by criminalizing the hardworking bussers and dishwashers who keep their restaurants open. Here in California, farmers are nearly as concerned about the lack of immigration reform as progressives, because strict immigration laws prevent farmers from employing a stable work force.[266]

Civil liberties. These can be framed to appeal to the high value that working-class whites place on privacy ("not spilling your guts") and their distrust of big government. Having a registry of Muslims is a classic example of government waste: 99.99% of Muslims aren't terrorists. What a waste of money to keep track of the God-fearing, law-abiding 99%—money better spent on tracking down the tiny fraction of people who are terrorists, Muslims or not.

Climate change. This is a hard one, but one thing is clear. Insisting that resistance comes from plebeians too ignorant to credit science frames this issue *precisely* in the way most likely to enlist working-class opposition to climate change initiatives. When I hear some environmentalists talk, I feel like I'm listening to my German Jewish grandmother calling Russian Jews peasants.

Climate change is too important to be sacrificed to snobbery. Rather than turning the climate change debate into a fight over the authority of science, why not enlist the support of farmers who see the changes on the ground as desertification sets in? "Who cares why it's happening?" one class-migrant climate activist advised. "Let's meet them on the ground. That's what they know, and they can see what's happening."

Policing and race. Perhaps no issue has proven more divisive in recent years than controversies over police shootings of African-Americans. This is an emotional and thorny topic. Here is my attempt to navigate it.

Black Lives Matter is an important movement because of the historic and continuing segregation and racism black people face in this country. Black men have been targeted by the police since policing was invented. It's disturbing that it took the cell phone to draw national attention to the issue of police violence against African-Americans. Many of us know young black men who have been pulled over time and again. The implicit association test documents the association of black people with violence, a stereotype that can escalate police encounters at warp speed.[267] "We laugh about how white perpetrators of mass murders manage to be captured alive time and time again," wrote a friend describing her reading group of 12 black women, while African-Americans meet death at the hands of the police for selling cigarettes. In Oakland, California, near my hometown, some police sent racist texts while others were involved in a sexual misconduct scandal involving an underage girl.[268] Baltimore police routinely violate constitutional rights, discriminate against African-Americans, and use excessive force, the Justice Department concluded in 2017.[269] Toxic organizational cultures exist. They need to change.

At the same time, police have a stressful and dangerous job, and most work hard to do a tough job well. There are a few bad apples, but the problem goes beyond that. There also is an institutional culture that communicates ... what exactly? That black men need to be immediately and consistently submissive? That if they don't they present an existential threat? That would help explain Eric Garner, but not the numerous men who have been shot as they ran away. Nor does it explain the way Sandra Bland was mistreated.

All true, yet we need to discuss these pressing issues without fueling populist rage more than necessary. I spoke with a lawyer who's a class migrant about the neighborhood where he grew up, in Staten Island, which voted heavily for Donald Trump:

> *It's full of New York City civil servants—fire fighters, cops, garbage men—and Trump spoke very directly to those people. Most people are working class and antagonistic to Black Lives Matter. People are scared for the cops. After Eric Garner, one guy walked up to two cops in Brooklyn and murdered them. He made a post on social media, and then went and shot them in the head. Many people I know hate [New York City Mayor] Bill de Blasio for the way he reacted to the Eric Garner thing. And police officers don't take kindly to people saying they are racist, terrible people. Neither side is giving honest credence to what the other side is saying.*

Shifting the tone of the debate about policing is similar to the shift I've seen in my lifetime in attitudes toward the military. When I was in my teens and images from the My Lai massacre were in the news, people spat on soldiers returning from Vietnam. Eventually we stopped. Some 40 years later, we now thank soldiers for their service. We thank them even though the military is still a very flawed institution where women soldiers fighting in Iraq were more likely to be raped by a colleague than killed by enemy fire.[270] We need to change destructive organizational cultures in both the military and the police, but at the same time we must respect the women and men who do the difficult and dangerous jobs that keep the rest of us safe.

One message with the potential to enlist white working-class support to end police violence against unarmed civilians is this: Police work is hard and dangerous work most of us aren't qualified to do. Having the courage, the composure, and the self-discipline to defuse potentially violent situations rather than escalating them—that's rare. Most people don't have what it takes. This argument also may help avoid situations where white juries side with the police even when the evidence suggests police have violated their own rules of engagement and constitutional norms.[271]

The bottom line is this. Business-as-usual in American politics means that class conflict is driving the country further and further from the mainstream, into deep wells of swirling fury. We need to defuse class conflict so we can return to common sense.

14

Why Are Democrats Worse at Connecting with the White Working Class than Republicans?

"ANYBODY GONE INTO Whole Foods lately and see what they charge for arugula?" Barack Obama asked a baffled Iowa audience during the 2008 presidential campaign. "I don't know what it is," a hospital clinic assistant confided to a reporter. "Maybe it's a Hawaiian thing."[272]

It's not a Hawaiian thing; it's an elite thing. The class culture gap is a huge driver in American politics today. Consider: Michael Dukakis had lettuce problems, too, when he discussed endive on the campaign trail. John Kerry meant to convey youthful fitness when he released a photo of himself wind-surfing; instead he communicated class privilege. Obama was derided for his awful bowling score.[273]

The class culture gap is driving politics in Europe, too. Three Dutch social scientists found that a pronounced increase in "cultural voting"—voting on family values and other cultural issues—accounts for most of the working class's shift to the right both in the United States and Europe. It is "not so much those with low incomes who are socially conservative but rather those who are poorly educated,"[274] they conclude, mixing important class insight with casual class affront.

Yes, politicians on the right occasionally suffer from this sort of class cluelessness as well—think of Mitt Romney's clumsy attempts to connect with working-class Midwestern voters by, for example, mentioning that his wife drives "a couple of Cadillacs," an American-made car.[275] But this kind of thing is more common on the left. An Iowa attack ad famously called Howard Dean a "tax hiking, government-expanding, latte-drinking, sushi-eating, Volvo-driving, *New York Times* reading, body-piercing, Hollywood-loving, left-wing freak show," which provides a thorough elision of PME folkways and Democratic politics.[276]

How did we get here? It started with a shift in the liberal coalition. The New Deal coalition, organized around economic issues, won the Democrats the presidency seven out of ten times between 1932 and 1968. That coalition was anchored by blue-collar workers, white Southerners, and African-Americans. But after passage of the civil rights legislation in the late 1960s and early 1970s, Democrats and white southerners parted ways,[277] and Democrats focused on building the other pillars of their coalition. In 1972, Democrats cemented this shift by nominating candidate George McGovern, who appealed instead to young college-educated activists.[278] Now Democrats are composed of two quite different factions, wrote *New York Times* columnist Thomas Edsall in 2006: "downscale" Democrats (minorities, union members, public employees, the poor) and "upscale" Democrats. Upscale Democrats include academics, librarians, psychologists, human relations managers, editors; in other words, they are the intellectual reform-minded elite, who often define themselves in opposition to the business-minded elite. "Although this well-educated, culturally libertarian, relatively affluent progressive elite forms a minority [40%] of the Democratic Party," noted Edsall, "it is this activist stratum that sets the agenda for the Democratic Party."[279] It was true in 2006, and it remains true today.

A crucial inflection point was the 1968 Democratic convention, which featured a violent confrontation between young protesters and Mayor Richard Daley's Chicago police. Here's how Bill Clinton described it: "The kids and their supporters saw the mayor and the cops as authoritarian, ignorant, violent bigots. The mayor and his largely blue-collar ethnic police force saw the kids as foul-mouthed, immoral, unpatriotic, soft upper-class kids who were too spoiled to respect authority, too selfish to appreciate what it takes to hold a society together, too cowardly to serve in Vietnam."[280]

The next step was for the Republican business elite to align with working-class whites. This alliance led Republicans to a defense of patriotism and family values, and with the rise of Ronald Reagan, to an overall hostility to government.

The role of big money in fueling all this is well documented.[281] But it's insulting, as Thomas Frank did in *What's The Matter with Kansas*, to depict the white working class as stooges duped by big money. Big money has been effective only because working-class whites have been persuaded.

This has left progressives scratching their heads. Liberals are mystified that working-class voters support tax cuts for the rich and benefit cuts for everyone else. But once you understand the class culture gap, conservatives' appeal makes more sense. Because the white working class resents programs for the poor, to the extent that benefit cuts target the poor, that's attractive. To the extent that tax cuts for the rich hold the promise of jobs, that's attractive, too. As unions' strength and reach diminished, their politicized view of structural class inequalities has been replaced by a sense that unions protect good jobs for the few, while capitalists provide good jobs for the many. Arlie Hochschild describes her growing realization: "Oil brought jobs. Jobs brought money. Money brought a better life." She describes the euphoria when a new business comes to town. "Pollution is the sacrifice we make for capitalism,"[282] mused one of her Tea Party friends.

As progressives' attention shifted to issues of peace and then equal rights and environmentalism, blue-collar workers felt abandoned. Sometimes they were: the Uber story provides an example. After taxi drivers paid $250,000 for taxi medallions (licenses that allow the holder to drive a cab), progressive San Francisco allowed Uber and other rideshare companies to break the laws taxis had to abide by, causing the value of medallions to plummet. Then the city issued even more medallions, further eroding their market value. Progressives in San Francisco had little interest in blue-collar cab drivers (many of them immigrant men of color); their solicitude was for "disruptive" companies run by the PME.[283]

Not only are blue-collar whites no longer the center of the progressive coalition, in some circles, they are no longer seen as part of it. In 2016 the Clinton campaign acted on the accepted wisdom that working-class whites were no longer even a part of the coalition. Bill Clinton warned repeatedly that Hillary's campaign needed to address working-class issues. But these warnings "fell on deaf ears" as he waged "a lonely, one-man war ... to appeal to working-class and white rural voters." His advice was "often dismissed with a hand wave by senior members of the team as a personal vendetta to win back the voters who elected him, from a talented but aging politician who simply refused to accept the new Democratic map," noted *Politico*.[284]

Why can't Democrats just ignore this group and count on their coalition of professional-class whites and minorities to deliver elections? That didn't work in 2016 and here's why: the Electoral College gives the white working class outsized political power. The Electoral College was designed to overweight the rural vote—today, that means working-class whites. We've all seen the electoral maps that show that vast interior of rural red rimmed by the thin blue lines of the East and West coasts. Unless hipsters move to Iowa, an infuriated rural electorate will continue to hold disproportionate power. For the 112 years of American history prior to the 2000 election, the candidate who won the popular vote also won the Electoral College vote.[285] In the five elections since, two Democratic candidates who won the popular vote have lost the Electoral College. The system is flawed, but it's the one we have.

The white working class is important not only for strategic but also for ethical reasons. Ideally, no politician should ignore whole swaths of the country. And the left professes to care about diversity and level playing fields. But they can barely look class issues in the eye.

In elections past, none of this mattered, because unions were influential in delivering white working-class votes for Democrats in key states, notably Michigan. But unions' strength has contracted, from a third of the workforce 50 years ago to 6.4% of the private workforce today.[286] The political impact of unions' decreased strength cannot be overestimated. And with unions so embattled, they have less money to fund massive get-out-the-vote efforts. In 2016, union leaders openly worried about Trump's strength even among union members. Most astonishing is that one out of five members of the American Federation of Teachers voted for Trump,[287] despite the Republican assault on teachers' unions, particularly in Wisconsin. Most of the country's largest labor unions endorsed Clinton as early as 2015, yet many union members voted for Trump. One article quotes a union member: "Growing up we were very strong Democrats, but the Democrat party left us," he said, and "the unions have left us, too."[288] Working-class whites blame not only government but also unions for the loss of good jobs.

Is this just "false consciousness"? Not really. The working class just wants what the professional elite already has: jobs that sustain them in their vision of a middle-class life. "The thing that really gets me is that Democrats try to offer policies (paid sick leave! minimum wage!) that would *help* the working class," a friend wrote me right after Trump was elected.

A few days' paid leave ain't gonna support a family. Nor is minimum wage. Working-class men aren't interested in working at McDonald's for $15/hour instead of $9.50. What they want is a job that paves the way to a modest middle-class standard of living. Trump was the first politician in a long time to promise that. Many voters deeply appreciated the fact that at least he understood what they need.

Conclusion

THIS BOOK DESCRIBES a relationship gone bad: that between the white working class and the PME. Empathy's a good place to start, but remedying this relationship will require more. Like all good family therapy, it will require not just that the family "troublemaker" learn to behave. What's amiss is the family dynamic that cast the "troublemaker" in that unhappy role. Changing that dynamic requires change on the part of the family members who are "not in the wrong."

It's a simple message: when you leave the two-thirds of Americans without college degrees out of your vision of the good life, they notice. And when elites commit to equality for many different groups but arrogantly dismiss "the dark rigidity of fundamentalist rural America,"[289] this is a recipe for extreme alienation among working-class whites. Deriding "political correctness" becomes a way for less-privileged whites to express their fury at the snobbery of more-privileged whites. If you like what that dynamic is doing to the country, by all means continue business as usual.

I don't, for two reasons. The first is ethical: I am committed to social equality, not for some groups but for all groups. The second is strategic: the hidden injuries of class now have become visible in politics so polarized that our democracy is threatened. Another key message is that elite truths don't make sense in working-class lives. Working-class truths do, and my hope is that I've provided a window into why. If we're not going to provide elite lives for the broad mass of people, neither can we expect them to embrace elite truths.

Once the elite cast the white working class outside of its ambit of responsibility, the elite did what elites do. They ignored those who print their *New York Times*, make their KitchenAides,[290] tell them at the doctor's to undress from the waist down. The professional class first stopped noticing, and then they started condescending. Class cluelessness became class callousness.

Much anxiety has been expressed about whether bringing the white working class into focus will mean that privileged whites will stop caring about racism. I think that remedying the relationship between the professional elite and working-class whites will actually help people of color. I recall a conversation with Angela Harris, an African-American law professor whom I was trying to interest in a joint conference on class. Angela, with her inimitable candor, told me I was describing an issue among white people. Implicit: not her business, but I should get on it. White-on-white crime, opined another friend in critical race theory.

Ignoring and belittling the white working class is not a constructive move vis-à-vis people of color. I suggest a different approach: one that condemns racism and builds an interracial coalition for economic justice. If you don't like how a family member behaves, the best approach is to assume that you need to establish a different relationship with them that brings out their better self. Typically that requires you to be your better self, too.

Less anxiety has been expressed on the gender front. This is ironic, given that women just suffered an historic setback. But sometimes an insistent focus on gender is not the best way to help women. Remedying the relationship between the PME and working-class whites will stop misogyny from being seen as a delicious poke-in-the-eye of the powerful.

I remain hopeful. Reckless alpha-male posturing, I suspect, will work about as well as it usually does: fine in the short term but poorly in the long term. Meanwhile, we need to begin the process of healing the rift between white elites and white workers so that class conflict no longer dominates and distorts our politics. We need to begin *now*.

Acknowledgments

Sarah Green Carmichael, my editor at *Harvard Business Review*, is the only reason I wrote my original Election Night article or this book. She clearly knows better than I do what I should write and when I should write it. She also knows how to improve my writing so it's readable. I owe her.

This book was written under hydraulic time pressure, and yet four people took time out of their busy lives to read it and give me comments. Suzanne Lebsock took a *lot* of time, saving me from gross errors of fact, judgment, and taste. It is not every author who gets a MacArthur-certified genius as a writing coach, historical consultant, and proofreader. I am humbled that this book got such close attention from someone whose writing skills far exceed my own.

Jennifer Sherman, whose work I admire and rely on a lot, also gave me unvarnished comments just when I needed them. So did Shauna Marshall, whose anxiety that focusing on the white working class will reinforce racial hierarchy I did not fully allay, but I tried. Thanks, too, to Michael

Mensah for reaching out to discuss the racial dynamic in Trump's election.

Heather Boushey and Kavya Vaghul of the Center for Equitable Growth recalculated, on short notice, median incomes and other data so I could update definitions of the professional elite and the working class; I really appreciate their work. My agent, Roger S. Williams, of Roger Williams Agency, is the best agent a girl could have. Lisa McCorkell stayed up until 2:20 am to give me crucial comments and feedback, and then she and Marina Multhaup worked 24/7 to make the cites spic 'n span (and accurate). Also supporting this large undertaking were Sonia Marton and Saima Ali. Hilary Hardcastle, my library liaison, provides the expert librarianship that has transformed my research life. Thanks to Frank Furstenberg, Nina Segre, and Linda Bialecki for reviewing the book on short notice. Thanks, too, to two old friends who helped me find stuff quick: Chris Foreman and Dorothy Ross.

My husband James X. Dempsey not only read this book and gave valuable comments; all of my thinking about the white working class reflects 40 years of conversations with him. My mother-in-law Ruth Dempsey kept my spirits up as only she can do. And my children kept me centered and down to earth. I love them very much.

Notes

Preface

    1. Joan C. Williams et al., *Climate Control: Gender and Racial Bias in Engineering?* Center for WorkLife Law and Society of Women Engineers, October 2016.

    2. This study used the résumés of 80 higher-class and 78 lower-class men; the candidates were identically qualified. It found that 16.25 percent of the higher-class men received interview invitations, but only one lower-class man did. Lauren A. Rivera and András Tilcsik, "Class Advantage, Commitment Penalty: The Gendered Effect of Social Class Signals in an Elite Labor Market," *American Sociological Review* 81, no. 6 (2016): 1097–1131.

    3. Mark Lilla, *The Once and Future Liberal: After Identity Politics* (New York: Harper, 2017).

    4. Economic Policy Institute, "The Productivity–Pay Gap," August 2018, https://www.epi.org/productivity-pay-gap/.

    5. Raj Chetty et al., *The Fading American Dream: Trends in Absolute Income Mobility Since 1940*, NBER Working Paper No. 22910, 2017.

    6. The number of the crimes reported to the FBI increased by 17 percent from 2016 to 2017, FBI, "2017 Hate Crime Statistics Released," November 13, 2018, https://www.fbi.gov/news/stories/2017-hate-crime-statistics-released-111318. According to a survey by the Pew Research Center, 56 percent of Americans say President Trump has made race relations worse; 65 percent say it is more common for people to express racist or racially insensitive views, with 45 percent saying this has become more acceptable. Juliana Menasce Horowitz, Anna Brown, and Kiana Cox, "Race in America

2019," Pew Research Center, April 9, 2019, https://www.pewsocial trends.org/2019/04/09/race-in-america-2019/.

7. Richard Feloni, "High-Profile Investors Like Jeff Bezos, Ray Dalio, and Meg Whitman Are Flocking to a $150 Million Fund Nurturing Startups in Overlooked American Cities," *Business Insider,* February 6, 2018, https://www.businessinsider.com/rise-of-the-rest -steve-case-jd-vance-2018-1.

8. James Manyika et al., *Jobs Lost, Jobs Gained: Workforce Transitions in a Time of Automation,* McKinsey Global Institute, December 2017.

9. Emily Badger et al., "Extensive Data Shows Punishing Reach of Racism for Black Boys," *New York Times,* March 19, 2018.

10. Kristi Berner, "Can Businesses Help Fix the Incarceration Crisis? Columbia Business School, April 30, 2018, https://www.8.gsb .columbia.edu/articles/columbia-business/can-businesses-help-fix -incarceration-crisis.

11. Michèle Lamont, *The Dignity of Working Men: Morality and the Boundaries of Race, Class, and Immigration* (Boston: Harvard University Press, 2000): 116–128.

Chapter 1

1. https://en.wikipedia.org/wiki/Married..._with_Children; https://en.wikipedia.org/wiki/Homer_Simpson.

2. Ruy Teixeira and Joel Rogers, *America's Forgotten Majority: Why the White Working Class Still Matters* (New York: Basic Books, 2000), 11. Teixeira and Rogers call the white working class the "forgotten majority," because "we haven't heard much about them of late and ... they are ... about 55 percent of the voting population" (p. x).

3. Ann Case and Angus Deaton, "Rising Morbidity and Mortality in Midlife among White Non-Hispanic Americans in the 21st Century," *Proceedings of the National Academy of Sciences of the United States of America* 112, no. 49 (2015): 15078–15083; J. D. Vance, *Hillbilly Elegy: A Memoir of a Family and Culture in Crisis* (New York: Harper, 2016), 51.

4. Noah Bierman and Lisa Mascaro, "Donald Trump Supporter in South Carolina: We're Voting with Our Middle Finger," *Los Angeles Times,* February 16, 2016, http://www.latimes.com/local/lanow/ la-na-trump-south-carolina-20160216-story.html.

5. Olga Khazan, "Middle-Aged White Americans Are Dying of Despair," *The Atlantic,* November 4, 2015, http://www.theatlantic .com/health/archive/2015/11/boomers-deaths-pnas/413971/.

6. Forsetti's Justice, "An Insider's View: The Dark Rigidity of Fundamentalist Rural America," alternet.org, November 22, 2016, http://www.alternet.org/election-2016/rural-america-understanding-isnt-problem.

7. Richard Sennett and Jonathan Cobb, *The Hidden Injuries of Class* (New York: W.W. Norton, 1972).

8. Mark Lilla, "The End of Identity Liberalism," *New York Times*, November 18, 2016, https://www.nytimes.com/2016/11/20/opinion/sunday/the-end-of-identity-liberalism.html?partner=rss&emc=rss&_r=o.

Chapter 2

9. Sam Grobart, "Everybody Thinks They're Middle-Class," *BloombergBusinessweek*, September 15, 2016, https://www.bloomberg.com/features/2016-america-divided/middle-class/.

10. "How Close Are You to the Top 1%?" cnn.com, http://money.cnn.com/calculator/pf/income-rank/.

11. Joan C. Williams and Heather Boushey, "The Three Faces of Work-Family Conflict: The Poor, the Professionals, and the Missing Middle," Center for American Progress (2010): 3, https://cdn.americanprogress.org/wp-content/uploads/issues/2010/01/pdf/threefaces.pdf.

12. For a description of the methodology used to calculate the income medians and ranges for the poor, the professional elite, and the working class, see Williams and Boushey, "The Three Faces of Work-Family Conflict" (data and method appendix), 74. Many thanks to Heather Boushey and Kavya Vaghul of the Washington Center for Equitable Growth for updating these figures with 2015 data obtained from the 2014 Current Population Survey Annual Social and Economic Supplement (dollar values adjusted for inflation using the Consumer Price Index Research Series available from the U.S. Bureau of Labor Statistics).

13. Rachel Zupek, "15 Jobs that Pay $70,000 per Year," cnn.com, August 27, 2008, http://www.cnn.com/2008/LIVING/worklife/08/27/cb.jobs.that.pay.70k/index.html?iref=nextin.

14. Bureau of Labor Statistics, "Occupational Outlook Handbook: Police and Detectives," U.S. Department of Labor, https://www.bls.gov/ooh/protective-service/police-and-detectives.htm.

15. Williams and Boushey, "The Three Faces of Work-Family Conflict," 3 (figures updated with 2015 data). Many thanks to Heather Boushey and Kavya Vaghul of the Washington Center for Equitable Growth for updating these figures with 2015 data obtained from the 2014 Current Population Survey Annual Social and Economic Supplement (dollar values adjusted for inflation using the Consumer Price Index Research Series available from the U.S. Bureau of Labor Statistics). One note: I follow the convention of sometimes referring to the working class as "blue collar," although many have pink-collar jobs (as dental hygienists or "the girl" in the front office of the tire shop) or low-level white-collar jobs (as postal worker, receiving clerk, salesperson of paper goods to restaurants). The low-level white-collar jobs are gleaned from Michèle Lamont, *The Dignity of Working Men: Morality and the Boundaries of Race, Class, and Immigration* (Cambridge, MA: Harvard University Press, 2000).

16. Willams and Boushey, "The Three Faces of Work-Family Conflict," ii. Many thanks to Heather Boushey and Kavya Vaghul of the Washington Center for Equitable Growth for updating these figures with 2015 data obtained from the 2014 Current Population Survey Annual Social and Economic Supplement (dollar values adjusted for inflation using the Consumer Price Index Research Series available from the U.S. Bureau of Labor Statistics).

17. Nate Silver, "The Mythology of Trump's 'Working Class' Support," *FiveThirtyEight*, May 3, 2016, https://fivethirtyeight.com/features/the-mythology-of-trumps-working-class-support/.

18. In fact, the median incomes of the Trump primary voters in swing states are close to the $64,000 median income we found for the missing middle in 2010: Michigan (Trump voters' median income: $61,000), North Carolina ($62,000), Ohio ($64,000), and Wisconsin ($69,000). In the primary, relatively wealthier Republicans mostly voted for Marco Rubio ($88,000) or Dennis Kasich ($91,000). Trump voters' medians were a little higher in Florida ($70,000) and Pennsylvania ($71,000). See Nate Silver, "The Mythology of Trump's 'Working Class' Support," *FiveThirtyEight*, May 3, 2016, https://fivethirtyeight.com/features/the-mythology-of-trumps-working-class-support/.

19. Nate Silver, "Education, Not Income, Predicted Who Would Vote for Trump," *FiveThirtyEight*, November 22, 2016, http://

fivethirtyeight.com/features/education-not-income-predicted-who
-would-vote-for-trump/.

Chapter 3

20. For a complex answer to this complex topic, see Mark Pauly, Adam Leive, and Scott Harrington, "The Price of Responsibility: The Impact of Health Reform on Non-Poor Uninsureds," NBER Working Paper 21565 (2015).

21. Joan C. Williams and Heather Boushey, "The Three Faces of Work-Family Conflict: The Poor, the Professionals, and the Missing Middle," Center for American Progress (2010): 9, https://cdn.americanprogress.org/wp-content/uploads/issues/2010/01/pdf/threefaces.pdf.

22. Other books that get at this problem are Joseph T. Howell, *Hard Living on Clay Street: Portraits of Blue Collar Families* (Long Grove, IL: Waveland Press, 1972); and Maria J. Kefalas, *Working-Class Heroes: Protecting Home, Community, and Nation in a Chicago Neighborhood* (Oakland, CA: University of California Press, 2003).

23. J. D. Vance, *Hillbilly Elegy: A Memoir of a Family and Culture in Crisis* (New York: Harper, 2016).

24. Lillian B. Rubin, *Families on the Fault Line: America's Working Class Speaks About the Family, the Economy, Race, and Ethnicity* (New York: HarperCollins, 1994), 94, 96–97.

25. Williams and Boushey, "The Three Faces of Work-Family Conflict," 7, 9, 36.

26. Ellen E. Kossek, et al., "Family, Friend, and Neighbour Child Care Providers and Maternal Well-Being in Low-Income Systems: An Ecological Social Perspective," *Journal of Occupational and Organizational Psychology* 81 (2008): 370.

27. Michèle Lamont, *The Dignity of Working Men: Morality and the Boundaries of Race, Class, and Immigration* (Cambridge, MA: Harvard University Press, 2000), 19–20. Andrew Cherlin argues that working-class guys now embrace self-actualization rather than self-discipline (Andrew Cherlin and Timothy Nelson, "The Would-Be Working Class Today," in *Labor's Love Lost: The Rise and Fall of the Working-Class Family in America*, ed. Andrew Cherlin [New York: Russell Sage Foundation, 2014]). No doubt some do. As hard living has claimed a larger percentage of the white working class, more working-class

whites may well eschew the self-discipline ideal documented by
Michèle Lamont and many others. Yet I remain convinced that its
aspirational hold remains strong for settled working-class families.

28. Alfred Lubrano, *Limbo: Blue-Collar Roots, White-Collar Dreams*
(New York: Wiley, 2005), 16–17.

29. Lamont, *The Dignity of Working Men*, 2000, 1.

30. Vance, *Hillbilly Elegy*, 75, 91, 92, 113, 123, 156.

31. Julie Bettie, *Women Without Class: Girls, Race, and Identity*
(Oakland, CA: University of California Press, 2003), 15.

32. Howell, *Hard Living on Clay Street*, 257.

33. Lamont, *The Dignity of Working Men*, 27.

34. Kefalas, *Working-Class Heroes*, 12.

35. Joan C. Williams, *Reshaping the Work-Family Debate: Why
Men and Class Matter* (Cambridge, MA: Harvard University Press,
2010), 165.

36. Jennifer Sherman, *Those Who Work, Those Who Don't: Poverty,
Morality, and Family in Rural America* (Minneapolis, MN: University
of Minnesota Press, 2009), 126.

37. John Tierney, "For Good Self-Control, Try Getting Religious
About It," *New York Times*, December 29, 2008, http://www.nytimes
.com/2008/12/30/science/30tier.html.

38. Vance, *Hillbilly Elegy*, 92; Linda Gorman, "Is Religion Good
for You?" National Bureau of Economic Research, http://www
.nber.org/digest/oct05/w11377.html.

39. Vance, *Hillbilly Elegy*, 94.

40. Jonathan Gruber cited in Vance, *Hillbilly Elegy*, 92.

41. Suzanne Lebsock, "Snow Falling on Magnolias," in *Shapers
of Southern History: Autobiographical Reflections,* ed. John B. Boles
(Athens, GA: University of Georgia Press, 2004), 291.

42. Arlie Russell Hochschild, *Strangers in Their Own Land: Anger
and Mourning on the American Right* (New York: New Press, 2016), 114.

43. Jonathan Rieder, *Canarsie: The Jews and Italians of Brooklyn
against Liberalism* (Cambridge, MA: Harvard University Press,
1985), 119.

44. Vance, *Hillbilly Elegy*, 139.

45. Sherman, *Those Who Work, Those Who Don't,* 57, 69, 70, 71,
73–74.

46. Lamont, *The Dignity of Working Men,* 46–51.

47. U.S. Census Bureau, "Who's Minding the Kids? Child Care Arrangements: Summer 2006, Table 4: Children in Self-Care, by Age of Child, Employment Status of Mother, and Selected Characteristics for Children Living with Mother: Summer 2006," http://www2.census.gov/topics/childcare/sipp/2006-detail-tabs/tab04.xls.

Chapter 4

48. Tex Sample, *Blue Collar Resistance and the Politics of Jesus: Doing Ministry with Working Class Whites* (Nashville, TN: Abingdon Press, 2006), 61.

49. Barbara Ehrenreich, *Fear of Falling: The Inner Life of the Middle Class* (New York: HarperCollins, 1989), 137.

50. Annette Lareau, *Unequal Childhoods: Class, Race, and Family Life* (Oakland, CA: University of California Press, 2003), 140, 217–220.

51. Bob Secter, "Walker's Anti-Union Crusade Pivotal to White House Run, Damaging to Labor," *Chicago Tribune*, July 28, 2015, http://www.chicagotribune.com/news/nationworld/ct-scott-walker-wisconsin-unions-met-20150727-story.html.

52. Michéle Lamont, *The Dignity of Working Men: Morality and the Boundaries of Race, Class, and Immigration* (Cambridge, MA: Harvard University Press, 2000), 103.

53. Reeve Vanneman and Lynn Weber Cannon, *The American Perception of Class* (Philadelphia, PA: Temple University Press, 1987), 86–87.

54. Julie Jargon, "Middle-Market Woes Inspire Starbucks's Bet on Luxury Coffee," *Wall Street Journal*, December 5, 2016, http://www.wsj.com/articles/middle-market-woes-inspire-starbuckss-bet-on-luxury-coffee-1480966895.

55. Richard Dawkins, *The God Delusion* (New York: Mariner Books, 2006).

56. Arlie Russell Hochschild, *Strangers in Their Own Land: Anger and Mourning on the American Right* (New York: New Press, 2016), 182.

57. Lareau, *Unequal Childhoods*, 146–151.

58. Sample, *Blue Collar Resistance and the Politics of Jesus*, 27.

59. J. D. Vance, *Hillbilly Elegy: A Memoir of a Family and Culture in Crisis* (New York: Harper, 2016), 226.

60. Suzanne Lebsock, "Snow Falling on Magnolias," in *Shapers of Southern History: Autobiographical Reflections,* ed. John B. Boles (Athens, GA: University of Georgia Press, 2004), 296.

61. Joan C. Williams, *Reshaping the Work-Family Debate: Why Men and Class Matter* (Cambridge, MA: Harvard University Press, 2010), 169–171.

62. Lareau, *Unequal Childhoods,* 62–63.

63. Mark Granovetter, *Getting a Job: A Study of Contacts and Careers* (Chicago: University of Chicago Press, 1974), 19.

64. Lamont, *The Dignity of Working Men,* 99, 108.

65. Donna Langston, "Who Am I Now? The Politics of Class Identity," in *Working-Class Women in the Academy: Laborers in the Knowledge Factory,* ed. Michelle M. Tokarczyk and Elizabeth A. Fay (Amherst, MA: University of Massachusetts Press, 1993), 72.

66. Lamont, *The Dignity of Working Men,* 95.

67. Jennifer Sherman, *Those Who Work, Those Who Don't: Poverty, Morality, and Family in Rural America* (Minneapolis, MN: University of Minnesota Press, 2009), 107–108.

68. Sherman, *Those Who Work, Those Who Don't,* 110, 112.

69. https://en.wikipedia.org/wiki/Avant-garde.

70. Edmund Burke and Isaac Kramnick, *The Portable Edmund Burke* (London: Penguin Classics, 1999), 259.

71. Williams, *Reshaping the Work-Family Debate,* 205.

72. Confidential interview (Harvard-trained public-interest lawyer), Washington, D.C., 1999.

73. Pierre Bourdieu, *Distinction: A Social Critique of the Judgment of Taste,* trans. Richard Nice (Cambridge, MA: Harvard University Press, 1984).

Chapter 5

74. Drawn from this list: http://unemployment-rates.careertrends.com/stories/21415/cities-with-highest-unemployment-rates#100-San-Luis-AZ.

75. Ronald S. Burt, *Structural Holes: The Social Structure of Competition* (Cambridge, MA: Harvard University Press, 1995), 143–144.

76. Alfred Lubrano, *Limbo: Blue-Collar Roots, White-Collar Dreams* (New York: Wiley, 2004), 108.

77. Mary Blair-Loy, *Competing Devotions: Career and Family among Women Executives* (Cambridge, MA: Harvard University Press, 2003), 1–2, 13, 34.

78. Blair-Loy, *Competing Devotions*, 34, quoting Vicki Orlando (corporate lawyer).

79. Michèle Lamont, *The Dignity of Working Men: Morality and the Boundaries of Race, Class, and Immigration* (Cambridge, MA: Harvard University Press, 2000), 110.

80. Cynthia Fuchs Epstein, Carroll Seron, Bonnie Oglensky, and Robert Sauté, *The Part-Time Paradox: Time Norms, Professional Life, Family and Gender* (London: Routledge, 1999), 22.

81. Marianne Cooper, "Being the 'Go-To Guy': Fatherhood, Masculinity, and the Organization of Work in Silicon Valley," in *Families at Work: Expanding the Bounds 5*, ed. Naomi Gerstel et al. (Nashville, TN: Vanderbilt University Press, 2002), 26.

82. Cooper, "Being the 'Go-To Guy,'" 9.

83. Lamont, *The Dignity of Working Men*, 115–116.

84. Emily Gipple and Ben Gose, "America's Generosity Divide," *Chronicle of Philanthropy*, August 19, 2012, https://www.philanthropy.com/article/America-s-Generosity-Divide/156175.

85. Capitol Heights: median income $71,114: https://datausa.io/profile/geo/capitol-heights-md/. Suitland: median income $56,951: https://datausa.io/profile/geo/suitland-md/.

86. Maclean: median income $188,639: https://datausa.io/profile/geo/mclean-va/. Bethesda: income $145,288: https://datausa.io/profile/geo/bethesda-md/; https://www.philanthropy.com/article/America-s-Generosity-Divide/156175.

87. Jennifer Sherman, *Those Who Work, Those Who Don't: Poverty, Morality, and Family in Rural America* (Minneapolis, MN: University of Minnesota Press, 2009), 80, 113.

88. Annette Lareau, *Unequal Childhoods: Class, Race, and Family Life* (Oakland, CA: University of California Press, 2003), 204.

89. Arlie Russell Hochschild, *Strangers in Their Own Land: Anger and Mourning on the American Right* (New York: New Press, 2016), 106.

90. Naomi Cahn and June Carbone, *Red Families v. Blue Families: Legal Polarization and the Creation of Culture* (Oxford, UK: Oxford University Press, 2010), 2.

91. Andrew Cherlin, *Labor's Love Lost: The Rise and Fall of the Working-Class Family in America* (New York: Russell Sage Foundation, 2014), 146.

92. Kathryn Edin and Maria Kefalas, *Promises I Can Keep: Why Poor Women Put Motherhood before Marriage* (Oakland, CA: University of California Press, 2005), 2.

93. Charles Murray, *Losing Ground: American Social Policy, 1950–1980* (New York: Basic Books, 1984), 133, 159–162.

94. Gianpiero Petriglieri, "In Defense of Cosmopolitanism," hbr.org, December 15, 2016, https://hbr.org/2016/12/in-defense-of -cosmopolitanism.

Chapter 6

95. Pierre Bourdieu, *The Logic of Practice* (Redwood City, CA: Stanford University Press, 1980), 58.

96. Camille L. Ryan and Kurt Bauman, "Educational Attainment in the United States: 2015," http://www.census.gov/content/dam/ Census/library/publications/2016/demo/p20-578.pdf.

97. John Schmitt and Heather Boushey, "The College Conundrum: Why the Benefits of a College Education May Not Be So Clear, Especially to Men," Center for American Progress, December 2010, 1, https://www.americanprogress.org/wp-content/ uploads/issues/2010/12/pdf/college_conundrum.pdf.

98. Oliver Wright, "Don't Wear Brown Shoes if You Want to Walk into City Job, *The Times*, September 1, 2016, "http://www .thetimes.co.uk/article/dont-wear-brown-shoes-if-you-want-to-walk -into-city-job-gfcvt2ql2.

99. J. D. Vance, *Hillbilly Elegy: A Memoir of a Family and Culture in Crisis* (New York: Harper, 2016), 212, 213.

100. Lauren Rivera and András Tilcsik, "Research: How Subtle Class Cues Can Backfire on Your Resume," hbr.org, December 21, 2016, https://hbr.org/2016/12/research-how-subtle-class-cues-can -backfire-on-your-resume.

101. "Some Colleges Have More Students from the Top 1 Percent than the Bottom 60. Find Yours," *New York Times*, January 18, 2017, https://www.nytimes.com/interactive/2017/01/18/ upshot/some-colleges-have-more-students-from-the-top-1-percent -than-the-bottom-60.html?hp&action=click&pgtype=Homepage

&clickSource=story-heading&module=second-column-region
&region=top-news&WT.nav=top-news&_r=2.

102. Suzanne Mettler, *Degrees of Inequality: How the Politics of Higher Education Sabotaged the American Dream* (New York: Basic Books, 2014), 5.

103. Lisa R. Pruitt, "The False Choice between Race and Class and Other Affirmative Action Myths," *Buffalo Law Review* 63 (2015), 1038, citing Thomas J. Espenshade and Alexandria Walton Radford, *No Longer Separate, Not Yet Equal* (Princeton, NJ: Princeton University Press, 2009), 97–98.

104. Amanda L. Griffith and Donna S. Rothstein, "Can't Get There from Here: The Decision to Apply to a Selective College," *Economics of Education Review* 28 (2009): 623.

105. Nicholas Hillman and Taylor Weichman, "Education Deserts: The Continued Significance of 'Place' in the Twenty-First Century," American Council on Education/Center for Policy Research and Strategy, 2016, 3–4, 6, http://www.acenet.edu/news-room/ Documents/Education-Deserts-The-Continued-Significance-of -Place-in-the-Twenty-First-Century.pdf.

106. Griffith and Rothstein, "Can't Get There from Here," 627.

107. Schmitt and Boushey, "The College Conundrum," 3, 8, 9.

108. Schmitt and Boushey, "The College Conundrum," 5.

109. Jillian Berman, "Here's How Much Student-Loan Debt Has Exploded Over the Past Decade," MarketWatch, October 27, 2015, http://www.marketwatch.com/story/the-average-student-loan-debt -grew-56-over-the-past-10-years-2015-10-27.

110. Schmitt and Boushey, "The College Conundrum," 4.

111. Rework America, *America's Moment: Creating Opportunity in the Connected Age* (New York: W.W. Norton, 2015), 200.

112. Renny Christopher, "A Carpenter's Daughter," in *This Fine Place So Far from Home: Voices of Academics from the Working Class*, ed. C. L. Barney Dews and Carolyn Leste Law (Philadelphia, PA: Temple University Press, 1995), 143.

113. Arlie Russell Hochschild, *Strangers in Their Own Land: Anger and Mourning on the American Right* (New York: New Press, 2016), 73.

114. Confidential interview, Washington, D.C., 1999.

115. John Sumer, "Working It Out," in *This Fine Place So Far from Home: Voices of Academics from the Working Class*, ed. C. L. Barney

Dews and Carolyn Leste Law (Philadelphia, PA: Temple University Press, 1995), 304.

116. Michèle Lamont, *The Dignity of Working Men: Morality and the Boundaries of Race, Class, and Immigration* (Cambridge, MA: Harvard University Press, 2000), 20.

117. Nancy LaPaglia, "Working-Class Women as Academics," in *This Fine Place So Far from Home: Voices of Academics from the Working Class,* ed. C. L. Barney Dews and Carolyn Leste Law (Philadelphia, PA: Temple University Press, 1995), 180, 181.

118. Stephen Garger, "Bronx Syndrome," in *This Fine Place So Far from Home: Voices of Academics from the Working Class,* ed. C. L. Barney Dews and Carolyn Leste Law (Philadelphia, PA: Temple University Press, 1995), 46.

119. Hephzibah Roskelly, "Telling Tales in School: A Redneck Daughter in the Academy," in *Working-Class Women in the Academy,* ed. Michelle M. Tokarczyk and Elizabeth A. Fay (Amherst, MA: University of Massachusetts Press, 1993), 293.

120. Garger, "Bronx Syndrome," 46.

Chapter 7

121. Annette Lareau, *Unequal Childhoods: Class, Race, and Family Life* (Oakland, CA: University of California Press, 2003), 238.

122. Joan C. Williams, *Reshaping the Work-Family Debate: Why Men and Class Matter* (Cambridge, MA: Harvard University Press, 2010), 166–167.

123. bell hooks, "Keeping Close to Home: Class and Education," in *Working-Class Women in the Academy,* ed. Michelle M. Tokarczyk and Elizabeth A. Fay (Amherst, MA: University of Massachusetts Press, 1993), 102.

124. Lareau, *Unequal Childhoods,* 2–3, 42, Table C4 on 282, Table C5 on 283, Table C6 on 284.

125. Referring to Frederick W. Taylor, the "Father of Scientific Management." For more information, see Jill Lepore, "Not So Fast," *New Yorker,* October 12, 2009, http://www.newyorker.com/magazine/2009/10/12/not-so-fast.

126. Laureau, *Unequal Childhoods,* 39, 62, 113.

127. Laureau, *Unequal Childhoods,* 48, 58.

128. "Return to Childhood 2008," *This American Life* (Chicago Public Radio broadcast, March 7, 2008).

129. Laureau, *Unequal Childhoods,* 251.

130. Making Caring Common, "Turning the Tide: Inspiring Concern for Others and the Common Good through College Admissions," 2016, 5, http://mcc.gse.harvard.edu/files/gse-mcc/files/20160120_mcc_ttt_report_interactive.pdf?m=1453303517.

131. Lauren Rivera and András Tilcsik, "Research: How Subtle Class Cues Can Backfire on Your Resume," hbr.org, December 21, 2016, https://hbr.org/2016/12/research-how-subtle-class-cues-can -backfire-on-your-resume.

132. Laureau, *Unequal Childhoods,* 45, 79, 80, 81.

133. Laureau, *Unequal Childhoods,* 45, 55–57, 76–77.

Chapter 8

134. C. Vann Woodward, *Origins of the New South, 1877–1913* (Baton Rouge, LA: Louisiana State University Press, 1951), 209–211.

135. David R. Roediger, *The Wages of Whiteness: Race and the Making of the American Working Class* (London: Verso, 2007).

136. Reuel Schiller, *Forging Rivals: Race, Class, Law, and the Collapse of Postwar Liberalism* (Cambridge, UK: Cambridge University Press, 2015), 240–244.

137. See "Poor People's Campaign," kingencyclopedia.stanford .edu/encyclopedia/encyclopedia/enc_poor_peoples_campaign.

138. Julie Bettie, *Women Without Class: Girls, Race, and Identity* (Oakland, CA: University of California Press, 2002), 173.

139. Rich Morin, "Exploring Racial Bias Among Biracial and Single-Race Adults: The IAT," Pew Research Center, August 19, 2015, http://www.pewsocialtrends.org/2015/08/19/exploring-racial -bias-among-biracial-and-single-race-adults-the-iat/.

140. Chris Mooney, "The Science of Why Cops Shoot Young Black Men," *Mother Jones,* December 1, 2014, http://www.motherjones.com/politics/2014/11/science-of-racism-prejudice.

141. Marianne Bertrand and Sendhil Mullainathan, "Are Emily and Greg More Employable Than Lakisha and Jamal? A Field Experiment on Labor Market Discrimination," *American Economic Review* 94, no. 4 (2004).

142. Joan C. Williams, Su Li, Roberta Rincon, and Peter Finn, "Climate Control: Gender and Racial Bias in Engineering?" 2016, 18–19, http://worklifelaw.org/pubs/Climate-Control-Gender-And -Racial-Bias-In-Engineering.pdf. (The comparison is with white men because white women experience prove-it-again bias triggered by gender; women of color experience it based on both race and gender.)

143. Joan C. Williams and Rachel Dempsey, *What Works for Women at Work: Four Patterns Working Women Need to Know* (New York: New York University Press, 2014), 311–313 (see studies cited in endnotes to Chapter 2).

144. Michèle Lamont, *The Dignity of Working Men: Morality and the Boundaries of Race, Class, and Immigration* (Cambridge, MA: Harvard University Press, 2000), 73, citing Roel W. Meertiens and Thomas F. Pettigrew, "Is Subtle Prejudice Really Prejudice?" *Public Opinion Quarterly* 61 (1997): 54–71.

145. Jonathan Rieder, *Canarsie: The Jews and Italians of Brooklyn against Liberalism* (Cambridge, MA: Harvard University Press, 1985), 59, 60, 63.

146. Lamont, *The Dignity of Working Men*, 59.

147. Lamont, *The Dignity of Working Men*, 1.

148. Peter Holley, "KKK's Official Newspaper Supports Donald Trump for President," *Washington Post*, November 2, 2016, https:// www.washingtonpost.com/news/post-politics/wp/2016/11/01/the -kkks-official-newspaper-has-endorsed-donald-trump-for-president/ ?utm_term=.afd5f711ec41; Theodore Schleifer, "Trump: Judge with Mexican Heritage Has an 'Inherent Conflict of Interest,'" CNN .com, June 2, 2016, http://www.cnn.com/2016/06/02/politics/ donald-trump-judge-mexican-heritage-conflict-of-interest/; Jeremy Diamond, "Donald Trump: Ban All Muslim Travel to U.S.," CNN.com, December 8, 2015, http://www.cnn.com/2015/12/07/ politics/donald-trump-muslim-ban-immigration/; TIME Staff, "Here's Donald Trump's Presidential Announcement Speech," *TIME*, June 16, 2015, http://time.com/3923128/donald-trump -announcement-speech/.

149. Gary Langer, Gregory Holyk, Chad Kiewiet De Jonge, Julie Phelan, Geoff Feinberg, and Sofi Sinozich, "Huge Margin Among Working-Class Whites Lifts Trump to a Stunning Election

Upset," abcnews.com, November 9, 2016, http://abcnews.go.com/
Politics/huge-margin-working-class-whites-lifts-trump-stunning/
story?id=43411948; Aaron Blake, "Who Likes President Obama
and Voted for Donald Trump? Lots of People," *Washington Post*,
November 16, 2016, https://www.washingtonpost.com/news/the
-fix/wp/2016/11/16/meet-the-pro-obama-donald-trump-voters
-there-are-plenty-of-them/?utm_term=.bfdcoed42bo5.

150. German Lopez, "Research Says There Are Ways to Reduce
Racial Bias. Calling People Racist Isn't One of Them," vox.com,
November 15, 2016, http://www.vox.com/identities/2016/11/15/
13595508/racism-trump-research-study.

151. David Broockman and Joshua Kalla, "Durably Reducing
Transphobia: A Field Experiment on Door-to-Door Canvassing,"
Science 352 (2016): 220–224.

152. Dawn Michelle Baunach, "Decomposing Trends in Attitudes
Toward Gay Marriage, 1988–2006," *Social Science Quarterly* 92, no. 2
(2011): 346–363.

153. Rework America, *America's Moment: Creating Opportunity in
the Connected Age* (New York: W.W. Norton, 2015), 193.

154. U.S. Department of Agriculture, Economic Research Service,
"Immigration and the Rural Workforce," https://www.ers.usda.gov/
topics/in-the-news/immigration-and-the-rural-workforce/.

155. Jennifer Sherman, *Those Who Work, Those Who Don't:
Poverty, Morality, and Family in Rural America* (Minneapolis, MN:
University of Minnesota Press, 2009), 129.

156. Lamont, *The Dignity of Working Men,* 89–90.

157. Arlie Russell Hochschild, *Strangers in Their Own Land: Anger
and Mourning on the American Right* (New York: New Press, 2016), 92.

158. Hochschild, *Strangers in Their Own Land,* 93.

159. Andrew Cherlin, *Labor's Love Lost: The Rise and Fall of the
Working-Class Family in America* (New York: Russell Sage Foundation,
2014), 170.

160. Arlie Hochschild, "Feeling Rules," *The Managed Heart:
Commercialization of Human Feeling* (Oakland, CA: University of
California Press, 1983).

161. Hochschild, *Strangers in Their Own Land,* 137, 145, 221.

162. Amy Chozick, "Hillary Clinton Calls Many Trump Backers
'Deplorables,' and G.O.P. Pounces," *New York Times*, September 10,

2016, https://www.nytimes.com/2016/09/11/us/politics/hillary
-clinton-basket-of-deplorables.html?_r=0.

163. Thomas Haskell, *Objectivity Is Not Neutrality: Explanatory Schemes in History* (Baltimore, MD: Johns Hopkins University Press, 1998).

164. Hochschild, *Strangers in Their Own Land,* 47, 124.

165. Hochschild, *Strangers in Their Own Land,* 118, 137, 145.

166. Hochschild, *Strangers in Their Own Land,* 218.

167. Hochschild, *Strangers in Their Own Land,* 22–23, 122.

168. Alexis C. Madrigal, "The Racist Housing Policy That Made Your Neighborhood," *The Atlantic,* https://www.theatlantic.com/business/archive/2014/05/the-racist-housing-policy-that-made-your-neighborhood/371439/.

169. Kristin Luker, *Dubious Conceptions: The Politics of Teenage Pregnancy* (Cambridge, MA: Harvard University Press, 1996), 134–174.

170. Forthcoming on www.biasinterrupters.org.

171. Martin Bennett, "Martin Luther King Jr. and the Struggle for Economic Justice," California Labor Federation, January 18, 2015, http://calaborfed.org/martin_luther_king_jr-_and_the_struggle_for_economic_justice/.

Chapter 9

172. "Text of Clinton's 2008 Concession Speech," *The Guardian,* https://www.theguardian.com/commentisfree/2008/jun/07/hillaryclinton.uselections20081; Meghan Keneally, "Hillary Clinton's Progress Trying to 'Shatter That Highest, Hardest Glass Ceiling,'" abcnews.com, November 9, 2016, http://abcnews.go.com/Politics/hillary-clintons-progress-shatter-highest-hardest-glass-ceiling/story?id=43420815.

173. Arlie Russell Hochschild, *Strangers in Their Own Land: Anger and Mourning on the American Right* (New York: New Press, 2016), 147.

174. Rachel Martin and Alec MacGillis, "Feeling Left Behind, White Working-Class Voters Turned Out for Trump," npr.org, November 13, 2016, http://www.npr.org/2016/11/13/501904167/feeling-left-behind-white-working-class-voters-turned-out-for-trump.

175. Susan Chira, "'You Focus on the Good': Women Who Voted for Trump, in Their Own Words," *New York Times*, January 14, 2017, https://www.nytimes.com/2017/01/14/us/women-voters -trump.html?_r=0.

176. John Cassidy, "How Donald Trump Became President-Elect," *New Yorker*, November 9, 2016, http://www.newyorker.com/news/ john-cassidy/how-donald-trump-became-president-elect.

177. Joan Williams, *Unbending Gender: Why Family and Work Conflict and What to Do About It* (Oxford, UK: Oxford University Press, 2000), 66.

178. Vicki Shultz, "Telling Stories About Women and Work," *Harvard Law Review* 103, no. 8 (1990): footnote 332 on p. 1835.

179. Arlie Russell Hochschild, *The Time Bind: When Work Becomes Home and Home Becomes Work* (New York: Holt Paperbacks, 1997), 88.

180. Lillian B. Rubin, *Families on the Fault Line: America's Working Class Speaks About the Family, the Economy, Race, and Ethnicity* (New York: HarperCollins, 1994), 93.

181. Beth Shulman, *The Betrayal of Work: How Low Wage Jobs Fail 30 Million Americans and Their Families* (New York: New Press, 2003), 19–20, 37.

182. Ruth H. Bloch, "American Feminine Ideals in Transition: The Rise of the Moral Mother 1785–1815," *Feminist Studies* 44, no. 2 (1978): 101, 113, 114.

183. Williams, *Unbending Gender*, 153.

184. Ann Crittenden, *The Price of Motherhood: Why the Most Important Job in the World Is Still the Least Valued* (New York: Picador, 2001), 12.

185. Jacqueline Jones, *Labor of Love, Labor of Sorrow: Black Women, Work, and the Family, from Slavery to the Present* (New York: Basic Books, 1985); Riché Barnes, *Raising the Race: Black Career Women Redefine Marriage, Motherhood, and Community* (New Brunswick, NJ: Rutgers University Press, 2015).

186. Hochschild, *Strangers in Their Own Land*, 22.

187. Jessica Bennett, "A Master's Degree in . . . Masculinity?" *New York Times*, August 8, 2015, https://www.nytimes.com/2015/08/09/ fashion/masculinities-studies-stonybrook-michael-kimmel.html.

188. Steve Reilly, "Hundreds Allege Donald Trump Doesn't Pay His Bills," *USA Today*, June 9, 2016, http://www.usatoday.com/story/

news/politics/elections/2016/06/09/donald-trump-unpaid-bills
-republican-president-laswuits/85297274/.

189. Joan C. Williams and Rachel Dempsey, *What Works for Women at Work: Four Patterns Working Women Need to Know* (New York: New York University Press, 2014), Preface, citing Diana Burgess and Eugene Borgida, "Who Women Are, Who Women Should Be: Descriptive and Prescriptive Stereotyping in Sex Discrimination," *Psychology, Public Policy, and Law* 5, no. 3 (1999): 665–692.

190. Williams and Dempsey, *What Works for Women at Work,* 60.

191. Pamela J. Bettis and Natalie G. Adams, "Nice at Work in the Academy," unpublished paper; Alice H. Eagly and Steven J. Karau, "Role Congruity Theory of Prejudice Toward Female Leaders," *Psychological Review* 109, no. 3 (2002): 573–598; Susan T. Fiske, Amy J. C. Cuddy, Peter Glick, and Jun Xu, "A Model of (Often Mixed) Stereotype Content: Competence and Warmth Respectively Follow from Perceived Status and Competition," *Journal of Personal and Social Psychology* 82, no. 6 (2002): 878–902.

192. Susan T. Fiske, Jun Xu, Amy J. C. Cuddy, and Peter Glick, "(Dis)respecting versus (Dis)liking: Status and Interdependence Predict Ambivalent Stereotypes of Competence and Warmth," *Journal of Social Issues* 55, no. 3 (1999).

193. Chris Cillizza, "Hillary Clinton Has a Likability Problem. Donald Trump Has a Likability Epidemic," *Washington Post,* May 16, 2016, https://www.washingtonpost.com/ncws/the-fix/wp/2016/05/16/hillary-clintons-long-lingering-likable-enough-problem/?utm_term=.47be8d000860.

194. Robb Willer, Christabel L. Rogalin, Bridget Conlon, and Michael T. Wojnowicz, "Overdoing Gender: A Test of the Masculine Overcompensation Thesis," *American Journal of Sociology* 118 (2013): Table 5.

195. Francine M. Deutsch, *Halving It All: How Equally Shared Parenting Works* (Cambridge, MA: Harvard University Press, 1999), 193.

196. Carla Shows and Naomi Gerstel, "Fathering, Class and Gender," *Gender & Society* 23 (2009): 179.

197. Jennifer Sherman, *Those Who Work, Those Who Don't: Poverty, Morality, and Family in Rural America* (Minneapolis, MN: University of Minnesota Press, 2009), 123.

198. Robin J. Ely, Pamela Stone, and Colleen Ammerman, "Rethink What You 'Know' About High-Achieving Women," *Harvard Business Review*, December 2014, 100–109.

Chapter 10

199. "Wolfgang Lehmacher, "Don't Blame China for Taking U.S. Jobs," fortune.com, November 8, 2016, http://fortune.com/2016/11/08/china-automation-jobs/; Ben Casselman, "Manufacturing Jobs Are Never Coming Back," *FiveThirtyEight*, March 18, 2016, http://fivethirtyeight.com/features/manufacturing-jobs-are-never-coming-back/; Mark Muro, "Manufacturing Jobs Aren't Coming Back," *MIT Technology Review*, November 18, 2016, https://www.technologyreview.com/s/602869/manufacturing-jobs-arent-coming-back/.

200. Farhard Manjoo, "A Plan in Case Robots Take the Jobs: Give Everyone a Paycheck," *New York Times*, March 2, 2016, https://www.nytimes.com/2016/03/03/technology/plan-to-fight-robot-invasion-at-work-give-everyone-a-paycheck.html.

201. Rework America, *America's Moment: Creating Opportunity in the Connected Age* (New York: W.W. Norton, 2015), 201.

202. Rework America, *America's Moment,* 203, quoting Suzanne Berger, with the MIT Task Force on Production in the Innovation Economy, *Making in America: From Innovation to Market* (Cambridge, MA: MIT Press, 2013), 188–189.

203. Nicholas Wyman, "Why We Desperately Need to Bring Back Vocational Training in Schools," forbes.com, September 1, 2015, http://www.forbes.com/sites/nicholaswyman/2015/09/01/why-we-desperately-need-to-bring-back-vocational-training-in-schools/#6fab5521465c.

204. Rework America, *America's Moment,* 200.

205. Michael M. Crow and Williams B. Dabars, *Designing the New American University* (Baltimore, MD: Johns Hopkins University Press, 2015), 274–275.

206. Rework America, *America's Moment,* 222, 251.

207. Rework America, *America's Moment,* 208, citing http://www.electricaltrainingalliance.org.

208. Rework America, *America's Moment,* 209.

209. Rework America, *America's Moment,* 165–167.

210. Rework America, *America's Moment,* 42–45.

211. Rework America, *America's Moment*, 44.

212. Rework America, *America's Moment*, 50.

213. Rework America, *America's Moment*, 51, citing James Manyika, Jeff Sinclair, Richard Dobbs, Gernot Strube, Louis Rassey, Jan Mishke, Jaana Remes, Charles Roxburgh, Katy George, David O'Halloran, and Sreenivas Ramaswamy, *Manufacturing the Future: The Next Era of Global Growth and Innovation* (McKinsey Global Institute, 2012), 80.

Chapter 11

214. "No Safe Place: Violence Against Women, Interview: Michael Kimmel, PhD," pbs.org, http://www.pbs.org/kued/nosafeplace/interv/kimmel.html.

215. Michael Greenstone and Adam Looney, "The Problem with Men: A Look at Long-Term Employment Trends," The Hamilton Project, December 3, 2010, http://www.hamiltonproject.org/assets/files/milken_reduced_earnings_for_men_america.pdf.

216. Arlie Russell Hochschild, *Strangers in Their Own Land: Anger and Mourning on the American Right* (New York: New Press, 2016), 141; Phillip Longman, "Wealth and Generations," *Washington Monthly*, June-July-August 2015, http://washingtonmonthly.com/magazine/junejulyaug-2015/wealth-and-generations/. (This describes prime-age men.)

217. Betsey Stevenson, "Manly Men Need to Do More Girly Jobs," bloomberg.com, December 7, 2016, https://www.bloomberg.com/view/articles/2016-12-07/manly-men-need-to-do-more-girly-jobs.

218. Rework America, *America's Moment: Creating Opportunity in the Connected Age* (New York: W.W. Norton, 2015), 125.

219. Rework America, *America's Moment*, 114, 134.

220. Claire Cain Miller, "Why Men Don't Want the Jobs Done Mostly by Women," *New York Times*, January 4, 2017, https://www.nytimes.com/2017/01/04/upshot/why-men-dont-want-the-jobs-done-mostly-by-women.html?_r=0.

221. Rework America, *America's Moment*, 154, 207.

222. Charles Purdy, "Surprising Jobs with $100K Salaries—After Only a Two-Year Degree," *New York Daily News*, February 12, 2012, http://www.nydailynews.com/jobs/surprising-jobs-100k-salaries-two-year-degree-article-1.1026210; Frances Romero, "How Much

Do Plumbers Really Make?" *TIME*, October 17, 2008, http://
content.time.com/time/nation/article/0,8599,1851673,00.html.

Chapter 12

223. The Cash for Appliance stimulus program offers rebates for
appliances up to $250 per appliance, as long as the appliances replace
an existing appliance and bought during a specific time period. See
Suzan Clarke, "Rebate Program Gives Up to $250 for Purchase of
New, Energy-Saving Appliances," abcnews.com, February 12,
2010, http://abcnews.go.com/GMA/Home/cash-appliances-rebate
-energy-saving-purchases/story?id=9814094.

224. Suzanne Mettler, *The Submerged State: How Invisible
Government Policies Undermine American Democracy* (Chicago: University
of Chicago Press, 2011), 37.

225. Chana Joffe-Walt, "Unfit for Work: The Startling Rise of
Disability in America," npr.org, http://apps.npr.org/unfit-for-work/.

226. Jennifer Sherman, *Those Who Work, Those Who Don't:
Poverty, Morality, and Family in Rural America* (Minneapolis, MN:
University of Minnesota Press, 2009), 69.

227. Joffe-Walt, "Unfit for Work."

228. Joffe-Walt, "Unfit for Work."

229. Mettler, *The Submerged State*, 21.

230. Bob Cesca, "Keep Your Goddamn Government Hands Off
My Medicare!," *Huffington Post*, September 5, 2009, http://www
.huffingtonpost.com/bob-cesca/get-your-goddamn-governme_b_
252326.html.

231. Hope Schreiber, "Trump Supporter Schooled on FB for
Thinking Obamacare and ACA Are Different," elitedaily.com,
January 10, 2017, http://elitedaily.com/social-news/trump-supporter
-schooled-facebook-obamacare-affordable-care-act/1746982/; Jason
Linkins, "News Flash! Obamacare and the Affordable Care Act Are
the Same Thing," *Huffington Post*, January 17, 2017, http://www
.huffingtonpost.com/entry/obamacare-affordable-care-act_us_
587ea7f6e4b0cf0ae880af9a.

232. Pew Research Center, "Beyond Distrust: How Americans
View Their Government," November 23, 2015, http://www.people
-press.org/2015/11/23/beyond-distrust-how-americans-view-their
-government/.

233. Pew Research Center, "Beyond Distrust."

234. Michèle Lamont, *The Dignity of Working Men: Morality and the Boundaries of Race, Class, and Immigration* (Cambridge, MA: Harvard University Press, 2000), 21.

235. For an example of how the FDA has protected us, see Michael Winerip, "The Death and Afterlife of Thalidomide," *New York Times*, September 23, 2013, http://www.nytimes.com/2013/09/23/booming/the-death-and-afterlife-of-thalidomide.html.

236. Gary V. Engelhardt and Jonathan Gruber, "Social Security and the Evolution of Elderly Poverty," NBER Working Paper 10466 (2004), http://www.nber.org/papers/w10466.

237. Health Care Financing Administration, "Medicare 2000: 35 Years of Improving Americans' Health and Security," July 2000, https://usa.usembassy.de/etexts/soc/medicare35.pdf.

238. "Medicare Part D: Prescription Drug Coverage for Seniors," center-forward.org, http://center-forward.org/medicare-part-d-essential-coverage-for-seniors/.

239. "Who Is Poor?" Institute for Research on Poverty, University of Wisconsin-Madison, http://www.irp.wisc.edu/faqs/faq3.htm.

240. Michael Neal, "A Cross-Country Comparison of Homeownership Rates," Eye On Housing, June 19, 2015, http://eyeonhousing.org/2015/06/a-cross-country-comparison-of-homeownership-rates/; Daniel Goldstein, "Why the Federal Government Now Holds Nearly 50% of All Residential Mortgages," MarketWatch, October 16, 2015, http://www.marketwatch.com/story/why-the-federal-government-now-holds-nearly-50-of-all-residential-mortgages-2015-10-16.

241. Pew Research Center, "Beyond Distrust: How Americans View Their Government," November 23, 2015, http://www.people-press.org/2015/11/23/beyond-distrust-how-americans-view-their-government/.

242. Consumer Financial Protection Bureau, "CFPB Orders Citibank to Pay $700 Million in Consumer Relief for Illegal Credit Card Practices," July 21, 2015, http://www.consumerfinance.gov/about-us/newsroom/cfpb-orders-citibank-to-pay-700-million-in-consumer-relief-for-illegal-credit-card-practices/.

243. Arlie Russell Hochschild, *Strangers in Their Own Land: Anger and Mourning on the American Right* (New York: New Press, 2016), 43, 52, 108.

244. Kate Baldwin, "One Thing the US Military Gets Right: Childcare," *Quartz*, March 26, 2015, https://qz.com/369740/one -thing-the-us-military-gets-right-childcare/.

245. Pew Research Center, "Public Trust in Government: 1958– 2014," November 13, 2014, http://www.people-press.org/2014/11/ 13/public-trust-in-government/.

246. Mettler, *The Submerged State*, 65, citing Benjamin I. Page and Lawrence R. Jacobs, *Class War?: What Americans Really Think About Economic Inequality* (Chicago: University of Chicago Press, 2009), 144.

247. Mettler, *The Submerged State*, 70, 117.

248. The CFPB announced on January 18, 2017, that they are filing a lawsuit against Navient (the country's largest student loan servicer) for cheating borrowers; see Maggie McGrath, "CFPB Sues Student Loan Servicer Navient for Failing Borrowers 'At Every Stage,'" forbes.com, January 18, 2017, http://www.forbes.com/sites/ maggiemcgrath/2017/01/18/cfpb-sues-student-loan-servicer-navient -for-failing-borrowers-at-every-stage/#5fa7094d477d.

249. Mettler, *The Submerged State*, 15.

250. http://www.itgetsbetter.org/. I recognize that different levels of government are involved in, for example, sewers. My goal is a civics lesson, not a lesson in the arcane details of public finance.

251. J. D. Vance, *Hillbilly Elegy: A Memoir of a Family and Culture in Crisis* (New York: Harper, 2016), 189.

252. Lamont, *The Dignity of Working Men*, 35.

253. Joan C. Williams, *Reshaping the Work-Family Debate: Why Men and Class Matter* (Cambridge, MA: Harvard University Press, 2010), 197.

Chapter 13

254. Jonathan Martin and Alexander Burns, "Democrats at Crossroads: Win Back Working-Class Whites, or Let Them Go?" *New York Times*, December 15, 2016, http://www.nytimes.com/2016/12/15/ us/politics/democrats-joe-biden-hillary-clinton.html?_r=0.

255. Jennifer Bendery, "Pick Any LGBTQ Rights Issue. Jeff Sessions Has Voted Against It," *Huffington Post*, November 22, 2016,

http://www.huffingtonpost.com/entry/jeff-sessions-lgbt-rights_us_
58346cd9e4b030997bc1524f.

256. Peter Holley, "KKK's Official Newspaper Supports Donald
Trump for President," *Washington Post*, November 2, 2016, https://
www.washingtonpost.com/news/post-politics/wp/2016/11/01/the
-kkks-official-newspaper-has-endorsed-donald-trump-for-president/
?utm_term=.0999655a2360.

257. Tami Luhby and Jennifer Agiesta, "Exit Polls: Clinton Fails
to Energize African-Americans, Latinos and the Young," cnn.com,
November 9, 2016, http://www.cnn.com/2016/11/08/politics/first
-exit-polls-2016/.

258. Jens Manuel Krogstad, Mark Hugo Lopez, Gustavo López,
Jeffrey S. Passel, and Eileen Patten, "1. Looking Forward to 2016:
The Changing Latino Electorate," Pew Research Center, January 19,
2016, http://www.pewhispanic.org/2016/01/19/looking-forward-to
-2016-the-changing-latino-electorate/.

259. Marcela Valdes, "'We're Looking at a New Divide Within
the Hispanic Community,'" *New York Times Magazine*, November 15,
2016, https://www.nytimes.com/interactive/2016/11/20/magazine/
donald-trumps-america-florida-latino-vote.html?_r=0.

260. Philippe Sands, *East West Street: On the Origins of "Genocide"
and "Crimes Against Humanity"* (New York: Knopf, 2016).

261. Arlie Russell Hochschild, *Strangers in Their Own Land: Anger
and Mourning on the American Right* (New York: New Press, 2016), 141,
quoting Phillip Longman, "Wealth and Generations," *Washington
Monthly*, June-July-August 2015, http://washingtonmonthly.com/
magazine/junejulyaug-2015/wealth-and-generations/.

262. Ben Casselman, "Inequality Is Killing the American
Dream," *FiveThirtyEight*, December 8, 2016, http://fivethirtyeight
.com/features/inequality-is-killing-the-american-dream/.

263. Nick Timiraos, "5 Questions on Trade Adjustment
Assistance," *Wall Street Journal*, June 15, 2015, http://blogs.wsj.com/
briefly/2015/06/15/5-questions-on-trade-adjustment-assistance/.

264. Joel Paul, "The Cost of Free Trade," *Brown Journal of World
Affairs* 22 (2015).

265. Kristin Luker, *Abortion and the Politics of Motherhood*
(Oakland, CA: University of California Press, 1984), *supra* note 12, at
194–195 (pro-choice women work), 195 (pro-life women less likely

to work), cited in Joan Williams, *Unbending Gender: Why Family and Work Conflict and What to Do About It* (Oxford, UK: Oxford University Press, 2000), 151.

266. Jennifer Medina, "California Farmers Short of Labor, and Patience," *New York Times*, March 29, 2014, https://www.nytimes.com/2014/03/30/us/california-farmers-short-of-labor-and-patience.html.

267. Jennifer L. Eberhardt, Phillip Atiba Goff, Valerie J. Purdie, and Paul G. Davies, "Seeing Black: Race, Crime, and Visual Processing," *Journal of Personality and Social Psychology* 87, no. 6 (2004): 876–893, http://fairandimpartialpolicing.com/docs/pob5.pdf.

268. Rachel Swan, Phil Matier, and Andy Ross, "Oakland Police Bombshells: Racist Texts, Latest Chief Steps Down," sfgate.com, June 18, 2016, http://www.sfgate.com/news/article/Latest-Oakland-police-chief-is-out-after-two-days-8310286.php.

269. U.S. Department of Justice, Civil Rights Division, "Investigation of the Baltimore City Police Department," August 10, 2016, https://www.justice.gov/opa/file/883366/download.

270. Jane Harman, "Rapists in the Ranks," *Los Angeles Times*, March 31, 2008, http://www.latimes.com/news/la-oe-harman31mar31-story.html.

271. James Pinkerton, "Hard to Charge: Bulletproof Part 3," *Houston Chronicle*, http://www.houstonchronicle.com/local/investigations/item/Bulletproof-Part-3-Hard-to-charge-24421.php.

Chapter 14

272. John McCormick, "Obama Talks Arugula—Again—in Iowa," *The Swamp*, https://archive.fo/I3RIU.

273. Bernard Weinraub, "Campaign Trail; For Quayle, a Search for Belgian Endive," *New York Times*, September 20, 1988, http://www.nytimes.com/1988/09/20/us/campaign-trail-for-quayle-a-search-for-belgian-endive.html; Kate Zernike, "Who Among Us Does Not Love Windsurfing?," *New York Times*, September 5, 2004, http://www.nytimes.com/2004/09/05/weekinreview/who-among-us-does-not-love-windsurfing.html; Sarah Pavlus, "Scarborough on Obama's 'Dainty' Bowling Performance: 'Americans Want Their President, If It's a Man, to Be a Real Man,'" Media Matters for America, March 31, 2008, http://mediamatters.org/research/

2008/03/31/scarborough-on-obamas-dainty-bowling-performanc/ 143050.

274. Jeroen van der Waal, Peter Achterberg, and Dick Houtman, "Class Is Not Dead—It Has Been Buried Alive: Class Voting and Cultural Voting in Postwar Western Societies (1956–1990)," *Politics and Society* 35 (2007): 415.

275. Zach Carter, "Mitt Romney Doubles Down on Cadillac Gaffe, Accuses Obama of Corruption," *Huffington Post*, February 26, 2012, http://www.huffingtonpost.com/2012/02/26/mitt-romney -cadillac_n_1302193.html.

276. Nick Anderson and Janet Hook, "Dean Is Targeted by Ad Campaign," *Los Angeles Times*, January 7, 2004, http://articles .latimes.com/2004/jan/07/nation/na-media7.

277. Philip Bump, "When Did Black Americans Start Voting So Heavily Democratic?" *Washington Post*, July 7, 2015, https://www .washingtonpost.com/news/the-fix/wp/2015/07/07/when-did -black-americans-start-voting-so-heavily-democratic/; and "The Civil Rights Act of 1964: A Long Struggle for Freedom: Immediate Impact of the Civil Rights Act," Library of Congress, https://www .loc.gov/exhibits/civil-rights-act/immediate-impact.html.

278. Mark Stricherz, *Why The Democrats Are Blue: Secular Liberalism and the Decline of the People's Party* (New York: Encounter Books, 2007), 5–6; Geoffrey Layman and John Michael McTague, "Religion, Parties, and Voting Behavior: A Political Explanation of Religious Influence," in *The Oxford Handbook of Religion and American Politics,* ed. Corwin Smidt, Lyman Kellstedt, and James L. Guth (Oxford, UK: Oxford University Press, 2009), 343.

279. Thomas B. Edsall, *Building Red America: The New Conservative Coalition and the Drive for Permanent Power* (New York: Basic Books, 2006), 16–18.

280. Stricherz, *Why the Democrats Are Blue,* 1.

281. Jane Mayer, *Dark Money: The Hidden Story of the Billionaires behind the Rise of the Radical Right* (New York: Anchor, 2016).

282. Arlie Russell Hochschild, *Strangers in Their Own Land: Anger and Mourning on the American Right* (New York: New Press, 2016), 71–72, 179.

283. V. B. Dubal, "The Drive to Precarity: A Political History of Work, Regulation, & Labor Advocacy in San Francisco's Taxi &

Uber Economies," *Berkeley Journal of Employment and Labor Law* 38 (2017): 73–130.

284. Amy Chozick, "Hillary Clinton's Expectations, and Her Ultimate Campaign Missteps," *New York Times*, November 9, 2016, http://mobile.nytimes.com/2016/11/10/us/politics/hillary-clinton -campaign.html; T. Becket Adams, "Bill Clinton's Lonely, One-Man Effort to Win White Working-Class Voters," *Washington Examiner*, November 12, 2016, http://www.washingtonexaminer.com/bill -clintons-lonely-one-man-effort-to-win-white-working-class-voters/ article/2607228; Annie Karni, "Clinton Aides Blame Loss on Every-thing but Themselves," *Politico*, November 10, 2016, http://www .politico.com/story/2016/11/hillary-clinton-aides-loss-blame-231215.

285. https://en.wikipedia.org/wiki/United_States_presidential_ elections_in_which_the_winner_lost_the_popular_vote.

286. Quoctrung Bui, "50 Years of Shrinking Union Membership, in One Map," npr.org, February 23, 2015, http://www.npr.org/ sections/money/2015/02/23/385843576/50-years-of-shrinking-union -membership-in-one-map; Bureau of Labor Statistics, "Economic News Release: Union Members Summary," U.S. Department of Labor, January 26, 2017, http://www.bls.gov/news.release/union2 .nro.htm.

287. Greg Toppo, "Teacher Unions Smarting after Many Members Vote for Trump," *USA Today*, November 23, 2016, http://www .usatoday.com/story/news/2016/11/23/election-unions-teachers -clinton-trump/94242722/.

288. Patricia Murphy, "Why These Union Members and Lifelong Democrats Are Voting Trump," *The Daily Beast*, July 26, 2016, http://www.thedailybeast.com/articles/2016/07/26/why-these -union-members-and-lifelong-democrats-are-voting-trump.html.

Conclusion

289. Forsetti's Justice, "An Insider's View: The Dark Rigidity of Fundamentalist Rural America," alternet.org, November 22, 2016, http://www.alternet.org/election-2016/rural-america-understanding -isnt-problem.

290. Joe Mont, "10 Things Still Made in America," *The Street*, October 18, 2011, https://www.thestreet.com/story/11279838/4/ 10-things-still-made-in-america.html.

Additional Reading

If you want to know more about the working class and you want to read one book . . .

- Michèle Lamont, *The Dignity of Working Men: Morality and the Boundaries of Race, Class, and Immigration.* Cambridge, MA: Harvard University Press, 2000.

If you want to read five more, add:

- Arlie Russell Hochschild, *Strangers in Their Own Land: Anger and Mourning on the American Right.* New York: New Press, 2016.
- Annette Lareau, *Unequal Childhoods: Class, Race, and Family Life.* Berkeley: University of California Press, 2003.
- Jennifer Sherman, *Those Who Work, Those Who Don't: Poverty, Morality, and Family in Rural America.* Minneapolis: University of Minnesota Press, 2009.
- J. D. Vance, *Hillbilly Elegy: A Memoir of a Family and Culture in Crisis.* New York: Harper, 2016.
- "The Three Faces of Work-Family Conflict," Joan C. Williams and Heather Boushey, 2010, available at https://www .americanprogress.org/issues/economy/reports/2010/01/25/ 7194/the-three-faces-of-work-family-conflict/.

If you want to know more, add:

- Julie Bettie, *Women Without Class: Girls, Race, and Identity.* Berkeley: University of California Press, 2002.
- Jonathan Cobb and Richard Sennett, *The Hidden Injuries of Class.* New York: Alfred A. Knopf, 1972.
- Naomi Gerstell and Dan Clawson, *Unequal Time: Gender, Class, and Family in Employment Schedules.* New York: Russell Sage Foundation, 2014.
- Joseph T. Howell, *Hard Living on Clay Street: Portraits of Blue Collar Families,* revised edition with a new Preface and Epilogue. Long Grove, IL: Waveland Press, 2017.
- Maria Kefalas, *Working-Class Heroes: Protecting Home, Community, and Nation in a Chicago Neighborhood.* Berkeley: University of California Press, 2003.
- Lillian B. Rubin, *Worlds of Pain: Life in the Working-Class Family.* New York: Basic Books, 1963.

If you want to read more about the professional elite:

- Barbara Ehrenreich, *Fear of Falling: The Inner Life of the Middle Class.* New York: Pantheon Books, 1989.
- Michèle Lamont, *Money, Morals, and Manners: The Culture of the French and the American Upper-Middle Class.* Chicago: University of Chicago, 1992.

Index

About the Author

Joan C. Williams is a Distinguished Professor of Law, Hastings Foundation Chair, and Founding Director of the Center for WorkLife Law at the University of California, Hastings College of the Law. Described as having "something approaching rock star status" in her field by the *New York Times Magazine*, she has played a central role in debates about women's advancement for the past quarter-century. Williams's pathbreaking work helped create the field of work-family studies and modern workplace flexibility policies.

Williams's work on social class has influenced scholars, policymakers, and the press. It includes her prize-winning *Unbending Gender: Why Family and Work Conflict and What to Do About It* (Oxford University Press, 2000) and *Reshaping the Work-Family Debate: Why Men and Class Matter* (Harvard University Press, 2010) and such widely read reports as "The Three Faces of Work-Family Conflict" (coauthored with Heather Boushey, 2010). Williams has played a central role in documenting how work-family conflict affects working-class families through such reports as "One Sick Child Away from Being Fired" (2006) and "Improving Work-Life Fit in Hourly Jobs" (2011). Her *Harvard Business Review* article, "What So Many People Don't Get About the U.S. Working Class," quickly became the most-read article in HBR's 90-plus-year history. In addition, Williams uses the findings of social science to create stable schedules for hourly workers, and interrupt implicit bias, at major U.S. companies (see www.biasinterrupters.org and www.stableschedules.org).

Williams has authored more than ninety academic articles and nine books, including her 2014 book *What Works for Women at Work: Four Patterns Working Women Need to Know* (New York University Press), coauthored with Rachel Dempsey and featured on LeanIn.org. She is one of the ten most-cited scholars in her field. Her work has been covered in publications from *Oprah Magazine* to *The Atlantic*. Awards include the Families and Work Institute's Work Life Legacy Award (2014), the American Bar Foundation's Outstanding Scholar Award (2012), the ABA's Margaret Brent Award for Women Lawyers of Achievement (2006), and the Distinguished Publication Award of the Association for Women in Psychology (2004; with Monica Biernat and Faye Crosby). In 2008, she gave the Massey Lectures in the History of American Civilization at Harvard.

Williams obtained a B.A. in History from Yale University, a Master's in City Planning from Massachusetts Institute of Technology, and a J.D. from Harvard Law School. She resides in San Francisco, California, with her husband James X. Dempsey. She enjoys hiking and spending time with her children, Rachel Dempsey and Nick Williams.